"Jim Lockard's new book, CREATING THE BELOVED COMMUNITY is an essential read for every spiritual leader, of any faith tradition. He takes us to new levels of leadership integrity and shows the path forward through the cultural changes that have affected every spiritual community. If spirituality and religion are to continue to be relevant as the 21st century progresses, we would all do well to heed Jim Lockard's advice. You would be well advised to add this brilliant book to your library – and then read it."
~ Rev. Dr. Kenn Gordon, Spiritual Leader, Centers for Spiritual Living

"Practical, timely, and oh so relevant, CREATING THE BELOVED COMMUNITY is a road map to leadership transformation. It essentially gives us a virtual tour of the journey and the terrain to be traversed. It provides insights and tips on not only what lies ahead but what we need to take and leave behind to both complete and enjoy the journey. The book calls us out, as it calls us up, to a new level of commitment and compassion requiring spiritual maturation. Just as Dr. Martin Luther King, Jr. reminds us, the establishment of the beloved community 'will not ride in on the wings of inevitability,' this book reminds us that there is work to be done that can actually be done, if approached with agape love and deep intent." ~ Rev. Deborah L. Johnson, author of *The Sacred Yes* and *Your Deepest Intent*

"The one constant, the North Star of every vital community is its commitment to nurturing a culture of love. This reverent commitment uplifts our relationships to one another and to the world at large. Without it, our collective experience is embittered rather than empowered. In Jim Lockard's masterful and pioneering new work, CREATING THE BELOVED COMMUNITY, we are shown how to consciously return to this self-existent cause of love and find ourselves uncovering healthy and possibility driven spiritual centers where the compassionate heart takes the lead." ~ Rev. Dr. David Ault - author of *The Grass Is Greener Right Here*

"This book and its content is extremely important in contributing to a world that works, for unity lives inside community." ~ Rev. Dr. Howard Caesar, Unity of Houston

"Anyone who leads a spiritual community of any faith, or a movement of any kind, must surely know about the challenges of navigating the ups and downs, obstacles and disappointments on the path. Jim Lockard's book provides relief, inspiration, and hope for those who are engaged creating a spiritual community. It takes the reader through a precise, deep, and uncompromisingly honest look at what leaders must face. CREATING THE BELOVED COMMUNITY ought to be required reading for anyone who desires to lead anyone else." ~ Rev. Dr. Edward Viljoen, author of Ordinary Goodness, and The Power of Meditation

"In CREATING THE BELOVED COMMUNITY, Jim Lockard brings two essential ideas to the field of spiritual leadership. The first, which Jim defines in a more significant and applicable way, is the need for authentic leadership. Role models who are entrusted with the spiritual well-being of others need to be immersed in integrity. The second is the application of the field of cultural evolution related to spiritual leadership - leaders are much more effective when they understand how changes in human culture affect spirituality and religion. This book will open your eyes, give you a new sense of connection with others and provide answers to today's questions. It is a must-read for anyone in spiritual leadership." ~ Rev. Dr. Temple Hayes, Unity Minister, Difference Maker, Author, International Speaker

"Where was THIS book when I was the spiritual leader of my church community for twenty-three years?" That is the question I found myself continually asking out loud as I read Jim Lockard's latest book, CREATING THE BELOVED COMMUNITY - A Handbook for Spiritual Leadership. This book belongs on every minister's bedside table as well as in every board room meeting. Things are changing rapidly and we need to stay current by introducing a new model for spiritual leadership because it is obvious that what worked fifty, thirty, twenty, or even ten years ago, doesn't necessarily work today. Whether you are a minister or lay leader, read this book carefully, and you'll discover that it really is a handbook to effective spiritual leadership for the 21st Century...and beyond!" ~ Dr. Dennis Merritt Jones, Award Winning Author of Your Redefining Moments and The Art of Being

Creating
The Beloved Community
A Handbook for Spiritual Leadership

Jim Lockard

Cover Photo of Sainte Chapelle, Paris: Jim Lockard

Cover Template by CoverDesignStudio.com

Author Photo Credit: Grace Stauffer Photography

Copyright © 2017 Jim Lockard

All rights reserved.

ISBN-10: 069272883X
ISBN-13: 978-0692728833 (Oneness Books)

DEDICATION

To my wife, Dorianne Cotter-Lockard, whose love and support lift me as a writer and as a human being. She is the perfect traveling companion on this journey through life. And to our daughters, Heather and Grace, who make life worth living and, quite often, show us how to live it.

TABLE OF CONTENTS

x

INTRODUCTION

*"Never try to force other people to accept Spiritual Truth.
Instead, see to it that they are so favorably impressed with your
own life and conduct, and the pace and joy that radiate from
you, that they will come running to you of their own accord,
begging you to give them the wonderful thing that you have."*
~ Emmet Fox

I do a good deal of coaching for spiritual leaders and consulting
with spiritual communities and organizations. I also have over 20
years of experience as a spiritual leader in four communities in
the United States. While each client is unique and each
community has its own culture and each organization has its own
history and vision, there is a common need that all share – finding
ways to fulfill the calling to bring positive spiritual principles to
both its members and the world at large.

In other words, how do we create and maintain what has been
called *The Beloved Community*?

I see *The Beloved Community* as people on a spiritual pathway
who seek a closer relationship with God (however named and
defined) AND as people who will take their spiritual awareness
into the world to be examples of love and compassion in action.
The Beloved Community is about being truly dedicated to walking
your talk – to being in full alignment with spiritual principles.

The nature of the individual pathway will vary. It can be the
teachings of any denomination of any faith tradition, or simply a
group of people who gather to find out how to be better versions
of themselves. A specific creed is important to each community,

of course, but almost any creed can be the seedbed of *The Beloved Community*.

If you have been a part of a spiritual community, whether housed in a church, synagogue, mosque, storefront, or under a tree, you have experienced teachings of love and compassion. You may have also experienced times when the community and its leaders did not live up to the ideals of love or compassion, or even when they expressed their opposites.

None of us is perfect; there will always be times when we fail to live up to high standards in any walk of life. In fact, such failures can be more important steps on the pathway to fully realizing the spiritual teachings that we seek to learn more fully. Given that there will always be failures of one kind or another, I see them relating to the concept of *The Beloved Community* in this way:

The Beloved Community has as a core mission to reveal and to heal such issues – to honestly confront them and to compassionately make corrections as they unfold. This core mission might be stated as *"To be in congruence with our highest values and to return to congruence quickly and surely when we fail to live up to those values."*

This is a book for those who are in spiritual leadership, or who aspire to be. That would include clergy, lay ministers, prayer ministers, and others who support the spiritual leaders in a local spiritual community or in a spiritual organization.

One great challenge of spiritual leadership is to engage members in the ongoing need to express spiritual principles at the highest level in their lives. After that, they need to develop the capacity to express those principles as a community. There is a dynamic tension between keeping people happy with the way things are done in any given community and being a true teacher of spiritual principles, which will involve leading students into discomfort. The spiritual leader's role is to encourage people in the direction of high expression, even though it is challenging for them to do so.

The capacity to stand in one's integrity and to teach students from that place of radical honesty is essential if a spiritual community is going to thrive as *The Beloved Community*. Congruence, with the spiritual principles of the community is critically important for alignment to exist. Living up to spiritual principles is always a challenge, calling forth qualities in people that may not be lived in any other way.

Seeking congruence with spiritual principles is a key element in the sense of integrity in any community. Members of *The Beloved Community* maintain integrity even in the face of apparent failure – by living their principles as fully as possible. My own faith tradition has a saying that "principle is not bound by precedent." This means that you can move into alignment with principle from any situation at any time.

Today, this challenging work must be done among people who live in evolving cultures with shifting values systems. New models have been developed in the past few decades that can help spiritual leaders to better navigate these changes which, to one degree or another, affect us all. The way that people relate to religion and spirituality is shifting and growing more complex. This book aims to assist spiritual leaders in better understanding some of these dynamics of change and to become more effective leaders in the process.

Leading a spiritual community is both demanding and fulfilling. Being in spiritual leadership involves a deep personal commitment requiring that one do his personal spiritual practices and engage in deep personal inquiry into his own beliefs, motivations, and shadow components. What is repressed and hidden within us can destroy our value as leaders and do great harm to those who look to us for guidance, succor, and spiritual education.

And what is hidden within us can also help us to create *The Beloved Community* and serve God, the planet, and its inhabitants at the highest levels. Our inner genius, when awakened and expressed, is the key to transforming lives for the better. This is why deep inner work is so important and must be done on an ongoing basis. One never quite arrives fully, for we are all works in progress.

The task of every spiritual leader is to do the inner work of self-discovery and self-transformation to be a clear vessel for the transmission of Spirit from potential into actuality. Unless we become healthy as leaders, the potential to take our communities in a destructive direction or to stagnation is ever-present.

This book is a guide through the processes of self-development and leadership development needed for one to serve as an effective spiritual leader and to create *The Beloved Community*. It is intended for anyone who is in spiritual leadership, or who someday seeks to be in a spiritual leadership position. In this book, we will explore together some of the external and internal obstacles to creating *The Beloved Community* and how to overcome them. We will also explore some new models for leadership that provide important added understanding and tools to the spiritual leader in today's increasingly complex world.

I see spiritual leadership as a high calling, one that requires one to give everything they have to give. I hope that in some way this book supports spiritual leaders in a greater realization of their potential to be positive and inspirational influences for good.

I am indebted to many people who, knowingly or not, helped me to write this book. My ministerial teachers included some very bright lights. Rev. Dr. William Taliaferro, Rev. Dr. Arleen (Bump) Austin, Rev. Dr. David Walker, Rev. Dr. Carleton Whitehead, Rev. Dr. James Golden, Rev. Dr. Sue Rubin, and Rev. Dr. Stuart Grayson, to list a few. Additionally, hours of conversations about ministry and spiritual community with Rev. Dr. Kenn Gordon, Rev. Dr. Deborah Gordon, Rev. Dr. Steve Gabrielson, Rev. Dr. Charles Geddes, Rev. Dr. David Leonard, Rev. Dr. Dennis Merritt Jones, Rev. Dr. Keith Cox, Rev. John McLean, Rev. Mike McMorrow, Rev. Dr. James Mellon, Rev. Linda Fisher, Barbara Fields, and Dr. Steven Brabant, among others. Also, I am indebted to the members of the Conejo Valley (California) Interfaith Association, who show harmony while traveling on different spiritual pathways.

Invaluable editing and proofreading assistance came from Rev. Dr. Maureen Hoyt and Mary DiVincenzo; they helped me focus and neutralized most of my poor grammatical habits.

And to the many people for whom I am proud to have been a spiritual teacher, counselor, and minister – some formally and some informally. You have given me perhaps the greatest gift of all, the opportunity to serve and to learn and to grow. My deepest desire is that I have contributed in some positive way to each of you in finding your own way forward as a spiritual being.

Note: Throughout the book, I interchange the "he" and "we" pronouns as a means of escaping to some small degree the sexist traditions of past literary practices.

1 THE BELOVED COMMUNITY

"Our goal is to create a beloved community, and this will require a qualitative change in our souls as well as a quantitative change in our lives."
~ Dr. Martin Luther King, Jr.

The Beloved Community is a collection of individuals who are learning how to love themselves, one another, and the universe. Regardless what name we give this idea, it is the same thing – the creation of the experience of belonging and experiencing the wonders of who we are individually and collectively. It is a place where purpose and passion meet, where we practice being the person we desire to be and support others in that effort. It is where our faith in spiritual principles is realized as true compassion and service. *The Beloved Community* is a strong attractor to those who seek spiritual realization. It is not a place of struggle but of continual progress toward a vision. That progress may have its ups and downs, but there is a sense of forward motion and of being involved in something vital.

The Beloved Community can be seen in several contexts. One is the universal sense of human community referred to by Dr. Martin Luther King, Jr. when he said:

> *"The end is reconciliation; the end is redemption; the end is the creation of the Beloved Community. It is this type of spirit and this type of love that can transform opponents into friends. It is this type of understanding goodwill that will transform the deep gloom of the old age into the exuberant gladness of the new age. It is this love which will bring about miracles in the hearts of men."*

And in this statement from The King Center in Atlanta:

> *"Dr. King's Beloved Community is a global vision in which all people can share in the wealth of the earth. In the Beloved Community, poverty, hunger, and homelessness will not be tolerated because international standards of human decency will not allow it. Racism and all forms of discrimination, bigotry, and prejudice will be replaced by an all-inclusive spirit of sisterhood and brotherhood."*

The great theologian Howard Thurman saw *The Beloved Community* as a coming together of all people, races, genders, and beliefs, into one universal humanity. This is *The Beloved Community* in the universal sense. This universal sense of *The Beloved Community* can be thought of as an overarching goal. It is the penultimate experience that we seek – that of peace and harmony for all.

Another level of *The Beloved Community* is at the local spiritual community, which is the focus of this book. This idea arises from the recognition that the consciousness of universal humanity is the result of the consciousness of many local communities.

> *"As within, so without. As above, so below."*
> *~ Ancient Hermetic Philosophy*

To contribute to a larger collective consciousness of *The Beloved Community,* the local spiritual community must focus on the development of spiritual awareness and more expanded consciousness of its members. In other words, it must be as healthy as possible and continually work toward getting healthier. It must act in ways to help its members realize their own loving and compassionate natures more fully and to help them express those natures in the world beyond the actual or virtual walls of the local spiritual community. And it must recognize our humanness, our tendency to fail along the pathway of learning. This is how the culture of the local spiritual community must manifest to be an authentic contributor to the *Universal Beloved Community*.

I suggest that the following qualities are important, even essential, to the creation and expansion of *The Beloved Community:*

- A consciousness of compassion

- A consciousness of love and connection

- A consciousness of deep and radical self-knowledge

- A consciousness of healing

- A consciousness of vision

- A consciousness of pioneering

- A consciousness of evolution and emergence

- A consciousness of mutual support

- A consciousness of contribution

- A consciousness of possibility

- A consciousness of resiliency

These qualities arise from the gathering of spiritually aware people who seek to deepen their realization through practice, learning, and connection. From these ideals and practices, *The Beloved Community* emerges – a community with something significant to contribute to the more universal beloved community. Committed people dedicated to the expansion of love and possibility constitute such a community.

There are a thousand ways that *The Beloved Community* can be structured. It is less about form than about function. The creation of spiritual community allows us to explore and actualize our developing selves within a spiritual context regardless of how we organize ourselves.

"A religious man is a person who holds God and man in one thought at one time, at all times, who suffers harm done to others, whose greatest passion is compassion, whose greatest strength is love and defiance of despair."
~ Abraham Joshua Heschel

Most spiritual communities are based upon the function of sharing a religious philosophy of life. People gather in community to learn the teachings and how to express them in their lives. In this way, the spiritual community is like an incubator – a place of safety and support for the kind of inner exploration needed to gain self-awareness and develop compassion. It is also very often a base of operations for outreach to the larger community and the world to be of service to those in need and to influence people for the better.

The Beloved Community is not only about dogma or belief, although they do inform the nature of each community; it is also discovering and actualizing the human sense of divinity to allow compassion to be expressed. Finding and nurturing the compassionate heart and living from that loving center is the ultimate goal of spiritual community. When that sense is realized, you are a part of *The Beloved Community*.

"The one and only test of a valid religious idea, doctrinal statement, spiritual experience, or devotional practice was that it must lead directly to practical compassion. If your understanding of the divine made you kinder, more empathetic, and impelled you to express this sympathy in concrete acts of loving-kindness, this was good theology. But if your notion of God made you unkind, belligerent, cruel, or self-righteous, or if it led you to kill in God's name, it was bad theology. Compassion was the litmus test for the prophets of Israel, for the rabbis of the Talmud, for Jesus, for Paul, and for Muhammad, not to mention Confucius, Lao-Tsu, the Buddha, or the sages of the Upanishads."
~ Karen Armstrong

There are many individuals who live from a compassionate heart. Some are part of a spiritual community and some are not. *The Beloved Community* is about those who seek to share with others the journey to the realization and the actualization of the compassionate heart. Each religious teaching will approach this process differently, as will each group of people who assemble for this purpose. Compassion, as the highest form of human expression, is always a part of the vision of a truly spiritual community.

When *the Beloved Community* shows itself compassionately in the world, it is a very powerful thing. It is something outside of the experience of most observers yet somehow recognizable. When members of an Amish community forgave a man who brutally killed several of their children, many were astonished. Such public acts of compassion are rare, as they arise from a consciousness that has transcended fear. Compassion is, therefore, at least in part, the transcendence of fear through the acceptance of the Divine and Divine Love.

Compassion is foremost the expression of divine love, endless love, a love that knows no restrictions or limitations. Such a love is available to all of us, but few manage to express it in their lives. In fact, few believe that it exists, much less that it is already within them. This expression of limitless love, its recognition and expression, is a desire of those within *The Beloved Community* and something they are always working to express in greater ways.

To be capable of true compassion – seeing the other as one with yourself – requires a degree of emotional and spiritual maturity. We must grow beyond our inherent fears and the conditioning that limits our ability to accept the wonders of divine love. A function of *The Beloved Community* is to foster the development of a mature emotional and spiritual self – to put away childish things and to become a true adult to transcend the limitations of fear and any sense of inadequacy. It is preparing ourselves to express our inner love and power more effectively in the world; and to assist our fellow community members in doing the same thing so that we develop *The Beloved Community* in the best sense possible.

It must be noted that every spiritual or religious community is not creating *The Beloved Community*. In fact, such communities are rather rare. This is because some spiritual communities do not teach how to develop the compassionate heart, nor do they teach the deep level of personal spiritual practice that is required for everyone to experience the personal psychological transformation necessary to awaken compassion in community members. The idea of the compassionate heart means, in part, developing a way of being where one is for something and against nothing. There is no external conflict arising from *The Beloved Community* – no need to make others wrong to feel better about themselves or their beliefs and practices.

The list of qualities mentioned earlier in this chapter is not meant to be a definitive list; it is what I have arrived at after giving the subject a great deal of thought. I see these qualities as being elements in the construction of a spiritual community that becomes *The Beloved Community* locally and which can contribute to the creation of *The Beloved Community* in the world.

Unless it is a contemplative community, *The Beloved Community* is not one that withdraws from the larger community nor is it one that sees itself as separate from everyone else. Rather, it engages with the world around it, but certainly not in spending energy making others wrong or in demeaning or diminishing others who are outside of the community. It is a place where differences may be noted, but in which the realization that all humans can live compassionate lives is very real.

The Beloved Community reflects a consciousness of pioneering, of evolution and emergence, where there is a recognition that the community will often find itself in uncharted waters, spiritually and socially. The sense of being a pioneering spirit, which is one who sets out to discover something new, leaving the comforts of the known behind, is an element present in such a community. A pioneering soul is one who explores her own spiritual nature with courage and a willingness to embrace the unknown. How else are we to leave the limited version of ourselves behind to make ourselves available to open to the emergence of a greater version of our divine potential?

Evolution and emergence mean that the community understands the nature of how we humans develop and change. They come to understand that all true change starts first on the inside and works its way outward into experience. That change within a dynamic community is often generated at the grass roots level rather than from the leadership. A major role of leadership is to nurture all this pioneering, exploring, evolving, and emerging into being – and to allow the disorder that goes along with all growth and change.

Connected to these qualities are those of contribution and resiliency. Giving is an essential part of spiritual community. The individual gives to others in many forms – attendance, participation, finances, spiritual practices, and other support. The community gives of itself both internally, to its members, and externally to the larger community in many forms – outreach programs, general volunteering, prayer support, financial support, and by being a presence of the spiritual community's philosophy in the larger world.

Resiliency is the capacity to handle setbacks, loss, and other challenges. This is a key element of spiritual community in general, and of *The Beloved Community* in particular. To be resilient is to realize that you have much to call upon when difficulties arise – both individually and collectively. Indeed, it is to hold a capacity for amazement and wonder regardless of what is in your immediate presence.

"Our goal should be to live life in radical amazement.... get up in the morning and look at the world in a way that takes nothing for granted. Everything is phenomenal; everything is incredible; never treat life casually. To be spiritual is to be amazed."
~ Abraham Joshua Heschel

Amazement is tied to the consciousness of healing, mutual support, and possibility, thus bringing the community forward to a greater capacity for compassion and love. The essence of *The Beloved Community* is just those things, and all the qualities in this chapter are essential elements to their realization. To be in *The Beloved Community* is to see with eyes of awe.

Another element to understand is that *The Beloved Community* can exist within a larger spiritual community where some or even many are not part of *The Beloved Community*. It can be very difficult, especially in a spiritual community with hundreds or even thousands of members, to see the kind of commitment and the level of participation necessary to create *The Beloved*

Community from everyone. However, it can consist of a subset of a larger spiritual community. It should not be "walled-off" from the larger community; its boundaries should be porous so that there is a freedom for those so motivated to come into *The Beloved Community* and for others to depart.

Spiritual leaders who recognize this will welcome those "cells of love" that such communities within a community create. Such groups become attractors to others and help to maintain the spiritual integrity of the larger spiritual community.

Of course, every spiritual community is a work in progress, changing over time. Within each community are people centered at a variety of developmental levels about each of these qualities. I will speak of other kinds of development and their impact in later chapters. It is important for spiritual leaders to recognize that their communities are always in flux, always changing; new people arrive as others leave; those present develop and grow or stay in place or even regress. There is always work to do.

The key is to hold and continue to communicate the vision of *The Beloved Community*, as well as its possibilities and its requirements, so that the spiritual community remains focused on the development of the compassionate heart – a heart that is open to the world.

"And now here is my secret, a very simple secret: It is only with the heart that one can see rightly; what is essential is invisible to the eye."
~ Antoine de Saint-Exupéry

2 OBSTACLES

"The value of a community depends on the spiritual and moral stature of the individuals composing it."
~ C.G. Jung

What obstacles arise in developing and living as *The Beloved Community*? Some of the major ones are:

- Our own developmental levels

- Our need for authority

- Our addiction to form

- Our limited skill sets

- Our own expectations

In other words, our humanness gets in the way. We come together as imperfectly actualized beings regarding the expression of our potential. Then, we try to grow spiritually in the company of others who mirror our imperfections back to us, triggering our negative patterns and bringing them to the surface. When we fail to see this, we may also fail to understand the fact that *The Beloved Community* unfolds AS us. Then we label what occurs as negative, and resist it instead of seeing that it is part of a process of growth.

When we come into community, we are recognizing the soul's call to commune with others in actualizing more of our potential to love and to be of deep service to creation. The fact that we seem to be so easily distracted from our soul's purpose by the dissonance of human interaction is one of the paradoxes of life.

The obstacles mentioned above are not the only obstacles, but they are commonly encountered when people are in spiritual community. I will explain each one to help you identify them and perhaps even avoid one or two along the pathway.

But before I do that, let me take this opportunity to mention that HOW we encounter the inevitable obstacles to *The Beloved Community* is equally important as whether or not we transcend them. The concept of spiritual poise – of being so grounded in practice that we become very difficult to unbalance – is critical. The idea is to encounter difficulties, which are after all inevitable, with grace and a sense of lightness. This is only possible when one has learned to keep a sense of spiritual poise as a core element of their identity. Complete victory over any obstacle is not necessary to live a fully spiritual life.

The first obstacle, *our own developmental levels*, refers to where each of us is along the spiral pathway of our psychological and emotional development. Have we developed beyond the stage of throwing tantrums? Are we like confident adults or fearful adolescents in our emotional reactions? Do we spend a lot of time and energy defending our ego needs (such as making sure that our rank or position is acknowledged)? Are we narcissistic? Do we offend easily? Do we crave power and attention? Are we dishonest with ourselves and others? Are we obsessive about controlling the way people behave or the way things are done?

Or have we grown beyond these stages to a greater sense of maturity and poise? Our various spiritual practices are designed to help us to move through to higher levels of development. Therefore, in communities where individuals are diligent in their spiritual practice and where that practice is seen in the context of human development, it is more likely that this obstacle will be both recognized and transcended.

"We have a fear of facing ourselves. That is the obstacle. Experiencing the innermost core of our existence is very embarrassing to a lot of people. A lot of people turn to something that they hope will liberate them without their having to face themselves. That is impossible. We can't do that. We have to be honest with ourselves. We have to see our gut, our excrement, our most undesirable parts. We have to see them. That is the foundation of warriorship, basically speaking. Whatever is there, we have to face it, we have to look at it, study it, work with it and practice meditation with it."
~ Chögyam Trungpa Rinpoche

Facing our own inner issues and demons is among the deepest spiritual and psychological work that we do. The purpose of such deep work is to transcend the negative fear-based beliefs that limit our expressions in life. The levels of development are simply indicators of how we are doing regarding this work. Our shadow-selves, the parts of us that we have repressed over time, hold us back from the expression of true, empowered love and the development of a compassionate heart. There is nothing wrong with any of the developmental levels. They are like the grades in elementary school, each one a building block toward the next, but the more we develop, the more we are likely to be poised and in dominion over our emotions. This is not about being tough, it is about being poised.

The obstacle which manifests from *our need for authority* is often one that attracts us to one community and repels us from another. The need (often unconscious) for external authority can be harmful in that we unconsciously project our needs onto an authority figure who may not be able to give us what we seek, or who may, out of his or her own lack of development, take advantage of us. Unresolved issues with our parents or other authority figures from our past are projected onto spiritual leaders – surely everyone who has served in the clergy in any form has experienced this – being the father or mother figure to members of the congregation. Understanding this dynamic and bringing it into awareness is an essential step in the healing process for all spiritual communities.

For spiritual leaders, a key aspect in the development of spiritual poise and maturity is coming to terms with our own sense of inner authority so that we can work in cooperation with others and serve in leadership from a place of personal love and authority. How we see ourselves in leadership and our relationship with other leaders is one of the areas of community that is most likely to be driven from our unconscious and repressed selves. Bringing these dynamics to consciousness is an essential aspect of healing ourselves and our communities, and it paves the way for the achievement of a mature spiritual way of being. There will be more on this in Chapter 3.

The obstacle which manifests as *our addiction to form* refers to our need to have our community look and feel a certain way for it to seem authentic to us. A great deal of energy often goes to keeping to an established form. This may be a necessity to some degree, but it is often given too much emphasis, drawing our energy away from more important things. For example, in a very traditional spiritual community, the form may be a core element of worship or of structure that is key to keeping faithful to the integrity of the teaching. On the other hand, there are many elements of form that are not integral to the spiritual teaching and may even get in the way of living as *The Beloved Community.*

The work of healing our attachments and addictions is deep soul work. We are usually unaware of our addictions to form. They are not like addictions to substances. They manifest differently. If we think of an addiction as any strong emotional attachment to something, one that the idea of changing or losing that thing triggers a strong emotional response, then we are identifying addictions to form.

"The way to healing an addiction lies in finding a connection between body and soul."
~ Marion Woodman

What types of forms might we be addicted to? Well, how the spiritual leader dresses for one. How the worship space is decorated; the order of service; what music is played during service; the brand of coffee served during fellowship; the times of the services, and so forth. Most spiritual leaders have experienced the challenges of changing these forms at some points in their careers. People can get upset about such things, and spiritual leaders can do damage to relationships with members either through their own or their members' excessive emphasis on form.

In times of great change, such as the time we are in now, the forms that remain the same can be a two-edged sword. They can comfort those who are threatened by the changing world around them; they can also be a hindrance to helping people to change with the times in positive ways. A healthy spiritual leadership may well see the difference and be able to facilitate the best outcome in such circumstances.

One aspect of an addiction, any addiction, is that it is not a rational attachment – it is an emotional or physical attachment. Therefore, reasoning about how changing the service times will make things flow better in the parking lot may not serve as an effective way to win people over. Some will just have to go "cold turkey" on the new service times. Human beings are emotional first, and we must learn to speak effectively to those emotions and develop a sense of emotional intelligence[1] if we are to mature successfully. Few areas of our personal growth as leaders are more important than our emotional intelligence level.

The obstacle which manifests as *our limited skill sets* relates to something other than our personal development or temperament or attitude. It relates to our possession of the knowledge, skills, and abilities needed to perform whatever tasks are needed to carry out our responsibilities – are we adequately prepared to do the job? Leaders throughout an organization need to know how

---

[1] Emotional Intelligence references abound. Do an online search or get the book **Emotional Intelligence** by Daniel Goleman, Bantam Books, 2005.

to lead and must understand the duties and responsibilities of those whom they lead. When the volunteer coordinator does not know how to recruit or organize volunteers, the resulting level of disharmony will require the energy and attention of others. Such distractions, when multiplied, can sidetrack the community from its mission. So, it is important to recruit skilled people and to train them on a regular basis so that things operate effectively. Competence is an element of spiritual growth.

Of course, this applies to the spiritual leaders of a community most of all. The skillset to be an effective spiritual leader is very broad. There are ecclesiastical skills, organizational skills, leadership skills, public speaking, counseling, and on and on. Few individuals will operate at a high level in all of these skills; therefore, ongoing education and personal development are essential in today's changing and more complex world. In addition, spiritual leaders need to recognize where their skillset is not the strongest and delegate those responsibilities where appropriate. How to delegate well is also an essential skill for leadership.

"We think that the point is to pass the test or overcome the problem, but the truth is that things don't really get 'solved.' They come together and they fall apart. Then they come together again and fall apart again. It's just like that. The healing comes from letting there be room for all of this to happen: room for grief and for relief, room for misery and for joy."
~ Pema Chödrön

The obstacle of *our own expectations* refers to those ideas that we have regarding how things should be or could be. Issues relating to this obstacle often occur when there is not a clearly communicated vision for the community, or when the community is mired in distractions due to issues relating to one or more of the other obstacles. Without a clearly articulated vision, competing voices will rise and, instead of a forward focus, current issues will take on outsized importance. Sound spiritual leadership is critical at this juncture. The spiritual leader who is clear and has done her own inner work can see past obstacles to a greater idea unfolding; she may even see the obstacle as an opportunity - something for which to be grateful and to put to good use as a learning tool.

"Don't be pushed by your problems. Be led by your dreams."
~ Ralph Waldo Emerson

When there is no clear vision for the community, it is important that one is developed, along with a mission statement, and a set of core values. It is best to invite as much input from the entire spiritual community as possible. There are expert facilitators who specialize in guiding this type of process who can be brought in to facilitate – but the spiritual leader cannot be hands-off in such a process. She needs to be championing the development of the vision both so that a high level of involvement is brought to bear and so that the vision gets traction once it is in place. She also needs to ensure that the developing vision, mission, and values are consistent with the spiritual philosophy of the community's faith tradition.

As I noted earlier, there can be many other obstacles to the development of *The Beloved Community*, but these are some of the most likely to be encountered. Other issues, such as insufficient resources and loss of membership, often stem from poorly managing one or more of the obstacles described above.

It is not that we expect no obstacles. It is that we expect to develop ways of being, in leadership and among the community in general, which allow us to encounter obstacles from a place of spiritual poise. Having done our preparatory work, we are now in possession of the necessary skills to transcend obstacles, learning our lessons along the way. This is all a part of a developmental pathway of developmental learning crucial to the creation of *The Beloved Community.*

This idea can then be taken to the next step, which is to see obstacles as gifts that allow something new to be called forth from within us; some new strength, skill, or level of compassion. This perspective is itself transformational, for instead of working to keep things from going wrong, we simply work toward the vison and treat any obstacles that appear as part of the process.

"The greatest and most important problems in life are all in a certain sense insoluble. They can never be solved, but only outgrown."
~ Carl Jung

An important stage in the development of a high-functioning spiritual community is to learn to see obstacles as gifts, because we may then realize that we have an infinite supply of strengths from within ourselves to draw upon. *The Beloved Community* is resilient, a quality which will only emerge when we are tested again and again. Spiritual leaders do well to keep this in mind when the inevitable challenges arise.

Our path is not the end but the way, and the path always contains elements to help us along the way. Sometimes these elements appear as positive experiences, sometimes as obstacles. Both are our teachers. New vistas of possibility open to us when we realize this truth. Failure to see the importance of vision or to focus on only what is in front of us limits our ability to realize our full potential.

We do not exist to solve problems, but to move toward a vision.

The Beloved Community is there as a vision and a guide to help us to be fulfilled in the expression of the best version of ourselves. It is both the path and the goal.

3 LEADERSHIP

"A leader must take special responsibility for what's going on inside his or her own self, inside his or her consciousness, lest the act of leadership create more harm than good."
~ Parker Palmer

A primary role of a spiritual leader, one who has prepared herself for such a role through rigorous study and practice, is to guide those in the community through the inevitable periods of dissonance in life. It is also to help people to recognize that a spiritual approach to life, while not preventing disharmony, does offer a way through to greater harmony. The spiritual leader does this through teaching the philosophy of the community and, more importantly, by being a living example of one who has integrated the philosophy into her life in a visible way.

As with the obstacle of too much attention to form that I wrote about in the previous chapter, we are often conditioned to expect to see spiritual community in a certain form – such as a churchlike building where Sunday services are held or a mosque for Friday evening prayers. We are conditioned (and sometimes required) to see credentialed leaders as the sole source of knowledge about the philosophy or teaching and are reluctant to question what we are told. This leads to a set of expectations that, if not managed properly, may sidetrack our progress toward creating *The Beloved Community*.

Leaders in spiritual communities often take on more responsibility than they can reasonably handle. This results in the kinds of ineffective leadership, and sometimes even abuse, that has affected too many spiritual communities. The leaders of spiritual communities must exemplify a challenging combination of confidence and vulnerability and must increasingly be more flexible than in the past.

"(Saint) Francis emphasized immediate experience and lifestyle: living in a different way. We were to live on the edge of the church in a very different lifestyle than simply running the church institution. In Franciscan theology, the best criticism of the bad is the practice of the better. Just go ahead and do it better. If you really believe in the values you say you believe in, then put them into practice. Don't waste any time trying to prove someone else is wrong or evil. As it states in the popular paraphrase of Francis' Rule, 'Preach the Gospel at all times, and when absolutely necessary, use words.'"
~ Richard Rohr

The acceptance of authoritarian leadership styles has evaporated in our culture to a significant extent. This evolutionary development requires leaders to do the inner work of building a more authentic and inclusive style of leadership. In *The Beloved Community*, no one is made to feel diminished by overly authoritarian leaders. Quite the opposite is true; leadership should empower those in the community by recognizing and encouraging the positive attributes within each person.

The kinds of leadership skills needed to create sustainable community extend beyond spiritual realization and personal leadership styles. Competent spiritual leaders create a variety of opportunities for others to flourish creatively and to contribute to the overall development of the spiritual community in every aspect of the organization. As Richard Rohr notes above, this must be done in a positive, proactive manner. We do not thrive by practicing avoidance nor by wasting our energy by disagreeing with or condemning others. We thrive by bringing our creativity and wisdom to bear on what we are creating, or more accurately, *co-creating* together, with humility and grace.

Competent leaders lead from a clear vision which they communicate effectively to others, and they ensure that everyone works in a coherent fashion toward the realization of that vision. Leadership also includes overseeing operational aspects, but it is really about being visionary, understanding people, possessing emotional intelligence, thinking systemically (seeing the big picture), and developing the leadership capacities of others. Vision always leads.

Spiritual Leaders are charged with the spiritual well-being of the community and usually charged with its administrative and organizational well-being as well. This requires an expansive skill set and a time commitment that can be daunting. The degree to which these various leadership responsibilities can be shared by others in the community is the determining factor in the sustainability of the community itself. While this is not always possible, it can be desirable in some cases. A spiritual leader who has become burned-out will drain energy from the community rather than bringing energy to it.

"There are two questions that we have to ask ourselves. The 1st is 'Where am I going?' and the 2nd is 'Who will go with me?' If you ever get these questions in the wrong order, you are in trouble."
~ Howard Thurman

The essential focus on spiritual and organizational leadership establishes the need to create a structure, an environment, and a presence in which *The Beloved Community* can evolve and thrive. In a spiritual community where dysfunction is the norm, the energy that could otherwise go toward developing the necessary consciousness to support the universal level of *The Beloved Community* goes instead to managing the dysfunction in that community.

Even when significant dysfunction is largely absent, incompetent leadership can result in a marginal level of functioning which requires most of the energy in the community to be devoted to organizational survival. Organizational aspects are important but secondary to the spiritual vision and mission of a spiritual community. You might think of the organizational aspects as the need to maintain your car. The more time you spend on vehicle maintenance, the less time you have to use the car for its true purpose – taking you where you want to go.

There are many cases where leaders lack one or more competencies of spiritual leadership despite what is considered sound training and preparation for their position. But just as often, I believe, the quality of the training and preparation is inadequate. There are many reasons for this, including the high cost of excellent training and education.

However, what seems to be frequently lacking in spiritual leadership development is the ability to show future spiritual leaders how to rigorously prepare themselves for their positions of leadership through thorough self-exploration, deep spiritual practice, and the development of a consciousness of scholarship. This needs to be followed up with a lifelong learning plan, both professional and personal, for spiritual leaders. Ongoing levels of accountability need to be in place, something that is often completely lacking after initial training programs end.

"You have to make people descend to the depths of themselves."
~ Svetlana Alexievich

When deep inner exploration is not facilitated, the unhealed shadow elements of the leader remain in place and are active in how she develops and actualizes her world view. Instead of leading people toward a greater realization of their soul natures, she will unconsciously use them as pawns in playing out the scripts of her unhealed wounds. We see this happen repeatedly in spiritual communities. The psychological well-being of spiritual leaders is an essential element of development and one that is too often overlooked.

"As long as the shadow remains unconscious and unrecognized it is at its most dangerous. Once we make the unconscious shadow conscious then we have the ability to work with it, to contain it and possibly even to transform it. It is consciousness which gives us choice; nothing can be transformed whilst it remains unconscious."
~ C.G. Jung

Spiritual leaders who have not done deep personal healing work may well be a danger to their community and to the larger society as well. The creation of *The Beloved Community* is all but impossible under such leadership. At best, such leaders guide their communities to a static place of marginal existence, always worried about having enough resources and experiencing infighting, gossip, and triangulation among the members. Or, they may thrive in terms of attendance and finances while building on people's shadow needs and creating an expanding reign of dysfunction that is often invisible to many in the congregation. In such cases the healthy members leave. People come into such a community unhealed, and they often leave with greater wounds than they had when they entered.

What are some of the symptoms of the presence of a leader with a heavy and unintegrated shadow-self?

- People may feel that they must walk on eggshells to avoid the wrath of the leader. In this case, an authoritarian personality style may develop where the spiritual leader consciously or unconsciously uses intimidation to manipulate others. For this to work over time, the leader will need to keep others from developing positive self-images. Those who show initiative or strength will be chastised and belittled. Note that such authoritarianism can look very pious in public but will change in private.

- People experience the leader as submissive and needy. He attracts people who are "rescuers," along with the occasional narcissist or sociopath who will tend to take over the community if given the opportunity. Gradually, over time, such leaders build a community of followers and enablers of the leaders' own dysfunctions. In fact, in such spiritual communities there is a high tolerance for dysfunction and victimhood. Those who are relatively healthy will see what is going on and eventually leave the community.

- The leader will continually have financial issues, both personally and within the spiritual community. This is not the occasional setback but a continual pattern of lack which is dealt with through manipulation, drama, and fear. Often, ethics are compromised when people in official positions are forced to take actions that are out of integrity to "support" the leader.

- The spiritual leader continually has relationship issues, both personally and within the spiritual community. This may manifest in romantic encounters or in who gets to be in the spiritual leader's "circle of friends." These are not real friendships, but sycophantic or co-dependent relationships which are more about power and insecurity than about love or friendship. Patterns of behavior unfold, and the community's second tier of leadership feels the need to keep the membership from knowing about it. The leader, with unresolved issues of self-worth or worse, may prey on newcomers using the leader's position of power and the intimacy that comes with being in a classroom or in "spiritual" counseling to compel compliance and silence.

- In all the above examples, co-dependency reigns, meaning that there are unconscious agreements to enable the various parties to keep their dysfunctions under wraps – except when someone becomes upset. Then there is a revelation that is destructive and usually very disruptive where some party is shamed. Then the co-dependence re-asserts itself, and everything is covered-up and not spoken of again – until someone else is upset enough to speak up.

- Spiritual leaders who have not done appropriate shadow work may also become addicted to their position as spiritual leader. It becomes an overwhelming emotional need to be seen in a certain light and treated a certain way. This addiction will likely include significant attachment issues regarding people and things. Nothing can be changed, no one can leave, or the spiritual leader goes into an emotional reaction or state that everyone has to rush in to help; or he simply disappears – announced or unannounced – for a period of time, all for dramatic effect.

"A codependent is a person, who at the moment of death, sees someone else's life flash in front of their eyes."
~ An Old Joke

The Beloved Community cannot be developed when situations such as these exist. Leadership must be in integrity, both personally and professionally. Nothing short of this will meet the standard necessary to motivate others to their highest level of inner integrity and outer performance.

Spiritual and religious organizations must take an active role in supporting and enforcing healthy behaviors among their spiritual leaders. Local spiritual communities are almost always ill-equipped to deal with spiritual leaders who are highly dysfunctional. This is true in no small part because dysfunctional spiritual leaders tend to seek to put their own enablers into positions of power so that they are protected.

"When we lack knowledge of our other side, we can do the most terrible things without calling ourselves to account and without ever suspecting what we're doing. Thus, we may be baffled by how others react to us. The increased self-knowledge that comes about through depth psychology allows us both to remedy our mistakes and to become more understanding and tolerant of others."
~ Daryl Sharp, Jungian analyst

Arriving at a positive and highly functional level of being is a shared responsibility. First, spiritual leaders need to see themselves as being solely responsible for their own spiritual and psychological health. Second, the credentialing and training organizations must recognize that they have the responsibility to teach students who will become spiritual leaders the importance of mental and spiritual health, to support leaders in displaying such health, and to support the spiritual communities of all leaders throughout the tenures of those leaders.

Effective spiritual leadership arises from several realized capacities within the leader. These include a sense of spiritual poise and maturity, which is developed during years of learning, experience, and spiritual practice. From that foundation of a healthy self, the competencies of leadership emerge.

Modern leadership recognizes the cultural evolutionary dynamics that affect spiritual communities, both at the local and cultural levels (addressed in Chapters 4 & 5). Evolutionary leaders know that psychological growth is developmental in nature and that a healthy psyche is essential to the achievement of spiritual maturity. Because leaders understand that spiritual growth in individuals takes the form of psychological transformation, they can inspire and encourage their members in this direction. The result is the development of a greater capacity to live from a compassionate heart throughout the spiritual community.

Another benefit is the development of the kind of insight to identify woundedness in others quickly. When the leader is healthy and lacks harmful ego needs, she is better able to facilitate healing in others. Unhealthy behaviors, which can arise from the unhealed woundedness of community members, are not encouraged or enabled by healthy leaders. When approached appropriately by a healthy spiritual leader, such behaviors tend to become extinguished over time – or the person may choose to leave the community rather than work toward their own healing.

People who have remained in a spiritual community long enough to understand the teachings of the faith tradition tend to leave for one of two reasons (other than simply moving from the area). They are either unwilling to do the deeper personal work on themselves to heal, or they have identified that the community leadership is unhealthy, and they are escaping. Either way, their departure can serve a valuable lesson to the spiritual leader about the community and its leadership.

When I was a spiritual leader, I normally had a policy in place that no newcomer could volunteer for any sacred service position in the community until they had been in attendance for a minimum of six weeks. What led me to adopt that practice was that I saw some newcomers who would unconsciously use immediate immersion into the volunteer/organizational part of the community as a way of avoiding the work of learning and practicing the principles on which the community was based.

This is often the person who may have commitment issues, so they tend to overcommit right away. They gush about the spiritual lesson after the service, pick up a copy of every brochure, sign all the volunteer sheets in the lobby and spend $150 in the book store. Often, you never see these people again – they literally scare themselves away out of fear of commitment. And if they do come back, they are prone to getting so involved that they quickly burn themselves out. This is usually out of a psychological need *not to commit* to anything, which can ironically show up as over-committing.

If I were in that position again, I would strongly consider extending that time to three or even six months. We are not in spiritual community to organize the community; that is a functional aspect that is done to support the true mission. We are in spiritual community to actualize our best selves and bring healing to a world that cries out for harmony. Our organizational practices should reflect a primary goal of bringing people into our faith tradition in the healthiest manner possible and to assist those people in working toward healthy spiritual and psychological development over time. Also, we should be thinking in terms of having people in volunteer positions who understand what we teach and who we are.

Evolved leaders, those who have done their personal work at depth, are good at manifesting and at attracting others who are also good at manifesting what is needed, so there is always enough of everything in terms of resources for the community to be sustained. Energy goes toward the vision and mission, with very little energy being applied to survival issues. An analogy would be riding a bicycle. Initially, all the new rider's attention and energy go into learning to balance and to move in the direction in which he wants to go. Once he has mastered that level, his attention moves to where he intends to go and very little goes toward the mechanics of riding.

So, it can be with basic organizational functioning – the spiritual leader focuses on the function initially and again from time to time when changes occur, but otherwise, his focus is on the vision and its unfolding. As the community grows, the organizational infrastructure will likely grow as well, although it is wise to keep from growing it too fast, so that people can be creative and contribute at a high level. You can accomplish more with a small group of properly prepared and motivated people than a large group that is not well prepared and motivated.

There is a symbiotic, or an attractive relationship between the spiritual leader and those who are attracted to her. When there is an absence of ego defense and a willingness to allow people to express their talents in the spiritual community, then healthy members are attracted. When the vision of the community is clearly communicated by the leadership and all activities and initiatives are designed to be coherent with that vision, the community thrives. There are no hidden agendas, no fragile leaders with egos to support, only a focus on the realization of the vision and mission.

I mentioned the need to develop the consciousness of scholarship earlier. By this, I do not mean that one needs to become an academic scholar, but I do think that one needs to develop the practices of good scholarship. These include diligent study of both the history of your field and what is emerging that is new, doing your homework on spiritual matters by continuing to gain knowledge of your faith tradition and its principles, and staying abreast of organizational matters by studying leadership and reading and committing to memory your own community's bylaws and policies and procedures. In other words, become fully prepared to do your job.

We are all called to be life-long learners in today's world. This is even more true of those in leadership positions. Learning never ends, and the need for well-informed and competent leadership never ends either. This is demanding to be sure but not beyond the capabilities of anyone committed to authentic spiritual leadership.

"Don't say you don't have enough time. You have exactly the same number of hours per day that were given to Helen Keller, Pasteur, Michelangelo, Mother Teresa, Leonardo da Vinci, Thomas Jefferson, and Albert Einstein."
~ H. Jackson Brown, Jr.

Evolutionary leadership, which recognizes and encourages the developmental nature of human growth, can be a powerful force for emerging good in the world. The leaders of the future are in many of our spiritual communities now — they need to learn to develop in a positive way toward the fullest realization of their inner gifts and talents so that they may someday serve the world at large. This too, is a function of *The Beloved Community*. I will address this further in Chapter 7.

Where the local spiritual community thrives with well prepared, spiritually mature leadership, *The Beloved Community* can arise and thrive.

4 CULTURAL EVOLUTION

"Is evolution a theory, a system, or a hypothesis? It is much more: it is a general condition to which all theories, all hypotheses, all systems must bow and which they must satisfy henceforward if they are to be thinkable and true. Evolution is a light illuminating all facts, a curve that all lines must follow."
~ Pierre Teilhard de Chardin, S.J.

The application of evolutionary theory to cultural development has opened new fields of inquiry across the many aspects of human culture. Here, our interest is in how evolutionary cultural development affects spiritual community, both at the macro level, or larger culture, and the micro level, within the local community itself. This cutting-edge inquiry is helping us to understand many of the factors affecting and changing how spiritual communities operate in the world.

In exploring the question – *is the basic synagogue/mosque/church model going away?* we find ourselves looking at a complex set of issues. The data[2] shows a drop in overall worship attendance in Europe, Australia, and North America that appears to be accelerating in recent years. However, there are several factors that affect how this overall trend manifests in various places, at various times, among various demographic groups, within specific denominations, and within individual spiritual communities.

A significant factor in this decline is that Sabbath days aren't what they used to be, especially in North America. This is particularly true for Sunday, which has been the Sabbath for the majority in North America over time. No longer an almost universal day of rest, it is for many people just another day of commercial activity and for some the only day for family activities. Sports leagues for children regularly schedule games and matches on Sunday morning – something that never would have happened a few decades ago. Now, it is rare for youth ministry leaders not to be missing some of their kids from Sunday youth programs during the months that these leagues are in action, not to mention the impact on youth attendance by uneven custody arrangements of divorced parents. Also, as worship attendance has declined, the concept of universal, social, and family pressure to attend services is, for many, largely a thing of the past.

I will note that this is not so much the case in most of Europe, where Sundays are still days when many businesses shutter their windows and lock their doors, and people do things with their families and friends. Yet, interestingly, worship attendance is far lower in Europe than in North America, as a rule. These are all effects of changing social patterns of behavior which are evolutionary in nature. There are other factors that both drive

---

[2] Pew Research America's Changing Religious Landscape (2015)
http://www.pewforum.org/2015/05/12/americas-changing-religious-landscape/

these social changes and arise from them. Let's look at a model that speaks to this kind of cultural evolutionary dynamic.

Spiral Dynamics™ is a model of human development which explores the complexity levels of human thinking and the value systems associated with those levels. Developed by Clare Graves, a professor at Union College in New York in the 1950's through the mid-1970's, the model grew out of Graves' desire to understand the psychologically healthy human being. The model proposes that increases in the complexity of human thinking have evolved over time in response to changes in the living conditions of human beings. As the outer world became more complex, increasingly, humans were driven to use more of their capacity to think in complex ways.

"What I am proposing is that the psychology of the mature human being is an unfolding, emergent, oscillating, spiraling process, marked by progressive subordination of old, lower-order behavior systems to new, higher-order systems as man's existential problems change."
~ Clare Graves

Grave's research, and the ongoing work that has been done by Don Beck and the late Chris Cowan, protégés of Graves, resulted in a model of a spiral showing increasing levels of human complexity. At one time, all early humans were very simplistic in their thinking, capable only of rudimentary survival strategies, finding nourishment, and mating – because that is all their cultural environment demanded of them. Today, we have massive metropolises, huge computer networks, scientific achievement in many areas – we have been to the moon! – as well as the ability to understand philosophy, create, play, and record beautiful music, and so much more.

What happened between those early humans, struggling for survival, and modern humans capable of such great achievement? Bio-social evolution happened. Within a modest degree of biological evolution came a massive degree of social and cultural evolutionary development, bringing humans individually and collectively to higher levels of operation and expression. And the spiral shows no signs of letting up. In fact, our rate of cultural evolution is picking up speed.

Here is a list of what are called the Levels of Existence on the Spiral according to the Spiral Dynamics Model (note that the colors themselves have no symbolic meaning):

Color	Description	When Emerged
Beige	Instinctual/Very Simplistic	Earliest Humans
Purple	Tribal/Communal/Rituals/Animism	30,000 years ago
Red	Egotistic/Individual/Power Gods	15,000 years ago
Blue	Traditional/Communal/Institutions	4,000 years ago
Orange	Scientific/Rational/Individual/Status	400 years ago
Green	Egalitarian/Communal/Emotions	75 years ago
Yellow	Integral/Individual/Very Complex	35 years ago
Turquoise	Holistic/Communal/Spiritual	20 years ago

Beige through Green are *1st Tier Levels of Existence*. Increasingly complex and alternately individualistic or communal, they have one thing in common – they are fear-based. Yellow and Turquoise represent the only identified 2nd Tier levels which have emerged as of today. The hallmarks of 2nd Tier are much greater complexity and the shift from a fear-based ego to a love-based ego or empowered sense of self.

As each level emerges in response to an increase in complexity in the world around the individual or group, not only does the capacity for complexity of thought increase, but values systems change as well. The more levels that are present, the greater the complexity of interaction. It is difficult for two people to fully understand one another if those people are two or more levels apart. Levels alternate between individualistic (self-serving – the warmer colors: Beige, Red, Orange, Yellow) and communal (self-sacrificing – the cooler colors: Purple, Blue, Green, Turquoise) value systems.

As a rule, a person will evolve to the level of the local group or community with whom they live. A child born in a place where Tribal-Purple is the dominant level will be taught from that perspective and will tend to develop to that level. It is possible for individuals to go beyond the level of the local culture on the spiral, although little is understood about that process. An increase in the complexity of the surrounding world is the driver for people to adapt to the more complex level of being. The adaptation to complexity emerges from within the person or group. When the Industrial Revolution occurred, millions left farms and moved to the cities, where life was more complex. Many adapted into Blue or even Orange in that process. Those who did not adapt had ongoing difficulties with living in a more complex society.

The Spiral Dynamics model is developmental, meaning that as one evolves up the spiral, one does not skip levels, although one may spend less time at one level than another. Each of us has a "center of gravity" or a dominant level from which we operate at any given stage of life; there may be some overflow, or more than one level may be active within a person at any given time. Additionally, we retain elements of any level that we have experienced in the past. This concept, in which levels we have left behind continue to influence us in the higher levels is called "transcend and include".

Today's societies in the developed West tend to be centered from Blue to Green on the spiral, with influences of Purple and Red showing up as well (remember Transcend and Include). There is also a small but growing number of people who are beginning to be centered at the 2nd Tier Levels of Integral-Yellow and Holistic-Turquoise. 2nd Tier levels of complexity are characterized by the absence of fear as a primary driver and the relinquishing of ego defenses. That may be where humanity's salvation lies, as the 1st Tier levels have created some problems that seemingly cannot be solved from 1st Tier levels of thinking.

"We cannot solve our problems with the same thinking we used when we created them."
~ Albert Einstein

There is much more to the Spiral Dynamics model, of course, and one should be cautious about applying it without some degree of knowledge of its intricacies and subtleties. Some guidelines:

- First, the levels are not discreet; that is, you exist in ALL of them all the time. However, you have a "center of gravity" that would include one or more levels that are close together on the spiral. That "center of gravity" moves in a developmental fashion. As each level emerges in the individual or group, the values of that level also emerge and become the operational values from which the worldview is constructed. Usually, we do not even recognize that we have changed, as it is an unconscious process.

- Second, higher levels on the spiral are not necessarily *better* than lower levels – what is important is that one's own level of development (color) be congruent with the level of complexity in the surrounding environment. There are times when someone operating at one of the "lower" levels will be much more effective at handling certain life conditions than someone at a more complex level. Clare Graves was very clear that "Everyone has a right to exist where they are," and that no person or organization should try to change the levels of anyone against their wishes.

- Third, the levels alternate between individualistic and communal worldviews – they alternate between "I" consciousness and "we" consciousness. For example, Orange is an individualistic level and Blue and Green, which surround Orange, are communal levels.

- Fourth, within each level or color, one can be either "Open," "Arrested," or "Closed," that is, one is on a continuum between being open to other ideas or ways of being or closed to them. This is a critical factor in how one deals with others in terms of tolerance and acceptance, and how easily one moves to a new level when one's living conditions demand it.

- Fifth, most people are not "centered" fully at any one level of existence, but may overlap two or more levels or become "stuck" between levels, which means that they have not fully progressed to the next level that is appropriate to the living conditions in which they find themselves.

- Sixth, the Spiral Dynamics model does not include aspects of being human such as intelligence, gender, race, or ethnicity; or things like whether one is an introvert or extrovert, abstract or analytical, cerebral or emotional.

Who, according to the model, are the most likely to be disenchanted with organized religion? Those who are farther up the spiral in terms of cultural evolution – those at Orange and Green in Spiral Dynamics terms, also known as the Moderns and the Cultural Creatives/Postmoderns.

The Modernist-Orange worldview is one of scientific-rational, individualistic, and often entrepreneurial thinking and values. The Traditionalist-Blue thinking and values are more centered in absolute right and wrong overseen by some Authority (The Bible, a king, a pope, an institution), are group oriented, and those at the Blue level of existence seek conformity and obey authority.

As the Orange level emerged more and more over time, its values began to dominate in the developed West. Democracy emerged because it gave the individual more freedom than a monarchy (which works better at Blue); science was unleashed to do research and exploration; business and entrepreneurship were elevated to higher status; people sought rational means to explain aspects of their lives, even seeing the universe as a Newtonian machine that would eventually be fully understood. If you are seen as being outside the prescribed values system, a person or organization operating at Traditionalist-Blue will punish you according to well-established rules, while those operating at Modernist-Orange may well celebrate your disruptive actions.

"The dogmas of the quiet past are inadequate to the stormy present."
~ Abraham Lincoln

People centered at the Modernist-Orange level continue to plunder the earth's resources as Blue had done, only with more powerful technology and less concern for others (remember,

Orange is individualistic). The dark side of Orange, often called "Toxic Orange," seeks wealth, status, and power above all else.

When a person centered at Orange comes into a spiritual community, whether healthy or unhealthy, they are interested in personal growth – success, how to get the best mate, to have prosperity, how to master the material aspects of life. They will want their names listed as major donors and want special attention for what and how much they give; Orange is a stage that values competition. They see this as perfectly normal and acceptable, as they are at a status and wealth-seeking stage of development. Bigger is better; richer is better. If you are seen as being outside the prescribed values, Orange may attempt to buy you out or bribe you into compliance, and failing that will try to marginalize your influence. Orange may also have some tendencies carried over from Red, meaning that they can get very nasty when blocked or crossed.

People centered at Orange will tend to view the concept of *The Beloved Community* from the position of how it might benefit them to participate and support the idea or goal.

Postmodernist-Green emerged in large numbers in the mid-20th century. Green thinking is communal, egalitarian, spiritual (but not religious!), and very concerned about feelings. For those centered at Green, feelings can supersede outcomes – one should only accept success if it makes everyone feel good, and it has personal meaning or is for the common good. People centered at this level will go to great pains to avoid hurting anyone's feelings. This is a more complex level than Modernist-Orange, and it carries with it a high rejection of the immediately preceding level (as all levels do at first).

Those centered at Green want intimacy, connection, authenticity, and healthy behaviors in their spiritual community. Green loves ritual (there is often a re-emergence of some aspects of Purple seen at this level). Green is non-judgmental except perhaps about perceived judgmentalism. Green abhors violence and manipulation, doesn't value competition with its winners and losers, but does value processes where every voice is heard. Green loves to be in community but is not particularly interested in formal membership or organizational structure or business. There is no rush to decide anything until some form of consensus is reached.

Green is likely to desire outreach or even activism for causes they hold dear – things such as peace, children's issues, equality, and the like. Those centered at Green are very enthusiastic about interfaith activities and interacting with local and national non-profits for good causes (many in the non-profit world are centered at Green). Green will gently lobby the spiritual leader to be more open and active about causes as well.

If you are seen as being outside the prescribed values, Green will attempt to use love to gently urge you into compliance and will take your non-compliance personally and emotionally. Those who are Toxic at Green may become absolutist in their views and the treatment of those who disagree with them.

Someone centered at Orange does not worship or participate in spiritual community the way that someone centered at Blue does, and Green doesn't do it like Blue or Orange. When those at each level attend a spiritual community, they attend for different reasons, and when they leave, they leave for different reasons. It is estimated that about 20% of the U.S. population is currently centered at Blue, about 40% is centered at Orange and 30% at Green. It is important to note that "centered" does not mean being exclusively at that single level. If I am centered at Orange that means that I am probably mostly at Orange and partly at Blue and partly at Green in my thinking and values. I may be mostly at Blue when it comes to my rules for someone dating my teenage daughter, at Orange as a sports fan and at work, and Green may be emerging in some areas. Someone's center of gravity can also be between levels, which means that they will be in a significant life transition internally and probably externally as well. There is a fluidity to the model that needs to be considered.

The Spiral Dynamics model does not explain everything about people. As noted above, it does not factor in such things as intelligence or whether someone is an introvert or extrovert. But it is useful in looking at those dynamics of human development which relate to complexity and the values associated with it, because our values drive our behavior.

On the positive side, people thinking at the Blue level gave us things like city-states, the great libraries and universities, social structures that worked, ethical constructs, flush toilets, and philosophy. People thinking at the Orange level took us to the moon, created the scientific revolution, built economic systems that created the most prosperity ever seen on the planet, developed a democracy that worked, and brought us the internet and your smart phone. People thinking at the Green level brought us the United Nations and UNESCO, the concept of ecology, fostered human and civil rights movements around the world, created human resources departments to encourage good treatment of employees, fostered deep meaning and connections in the world of work and art, promoted the "feminine" qualities of empathy, cooperation, and reconciliation in leadership, among many other things.

Each of these levels has both positive and negative aspects; they emerge when they are called forth by changing environments, and they fade (but do not disappear – remember transcend and include) when greater complexity calls the next level into expression. This ongoing process is clearly accelerating as the rate of cultural evolutionary change in human cultures is speeding up. There is no sign of a return to a relatively peaceful and static time, at least not anytime soon.

We have dipped our toes into Spiral Dynamics a bit here to make the point that these levels identified by colors represent different value systems which have emerged over time in human evolution, both individual and societal. New levels of thinking driven by the world around us becoming more complex, appear in response to that complexity. The three levels emphasized here – Traditionalist-Blue, Modernist-Orange, and Postmodernist-Green, are the dominant levels in North America, Australia, Europe, Japan, and some other places today. They are probably all present in your spiritual community.

"The primary motivators of people are the needs of the psychological stage they are inhabiting. The secondary motivators of people are the unmet needs of the psychological stages they have passed through."
~ Richard Barrett, Barrett Values Systems

Understanding these levels of existence, as they are called, helps us to understand some of the dynamics that affect how we are with one another and what the people in our larger communities are like in their evolutionary development. Remember, Spiral Dynamics is not primarily about the levels – it is about the dynamics that exist within and between the levels, and which, in fact, create the levels. These dynamics are developmental and evolutionary in nature, and they have a huge impact on what the worship activities and spiritual communities of our time look like.

When the leader of a spiritual community has no awareness of models like Spiral Dynamics and what they can convey, he will tend to unconsciously decide that anyone displaying values from levels on the spiral different than his own are bad or wrong. The result will either be a membership with values very much like the leader or a community with continual conflicts about values. This is simply a predictable result of a lack of awareness of evolutionary development and values systems and how they work.

Many spiritual communities are alike in their level on the spiral. Fundamentalist communities are centered at Blue – they are absolutist and literal in their thinking and world view. There is clarity about right and wrong, and there are very likely written rules and procedures to govern members in almost any eventuality. They are usually not open to different value systems. When individuals within a Blue-centered community evolve to the Orange level, it often becomes clear to them that they should leave the spiritual community, or they are asked to do so.

When the spiritual leader and much of the membership is centered at Orange, the spiritual community will be focused on growth, both personal and organizational. They want their place of worship to be big and, probably, technologically sophisticated. Many suburban megachurches in the U.S. are culturally centered at the Orange level.

The theological lessons of many of these Orange megachurches will be very close to those at a Blue-centered community but will tend to view wealth and prosperity as a good thing. Relativism begins to appear at the Orange level, so the spiritual message is softened a bit. The spiritual leader will likely be a lone individual, often unaffiliated with a larger denomination, and the community will very likely be personality driven. Status is important here, as is the focus on individual growth. Such communities may be very wealthy and make great displays of recognizing big donors.

When the spiritual leader and much of the membership is centered at Green, they are usually open and relativistic in their thinking. They want everyone to join their group as they value diversity. However, when they are unaware of the evolutionary dynamics involved, they will unconsciously do things that make people centered at other levels feel unwelcome. For example, a mom in the Blue/Orange range may bring a platter of homemade cupcakes for youth ministry snacks and be told that only "healthy" foods are welcome.

When people become centered at Green, they will have a higher level of rejection of Orange. This is likely to include leaving the "rat race" of corporate life and finding some alternative way of making an income. As noted above, they are less concerned with being seen as official members of an organization and have a negative view of hierarchy. This means that their level of giving may be lower than when they were centered at Blue or Orange, and their level of participation may be less because they are more likely to be sampling other spiritual communities and technologies, both online and off-line. As a spiritual community moves into Green, there is often a combination of reduced revenues, lower participation, and values conflict with those who remain at Orange or Blue.

"We are not going in circles; we are going upwards. The path is a spiral; we have already climbed many steps."
~ Hermann Hesse

Wherever we are centered on the spiral, we assume that our own values are the correct ones and other values are somehow aberrant or wrong. This is so even though our own values have changed as we moved along the spiral, but we were probably unaware of this for the most part. And remember, the first six levels through Green are fear-based ways of thinking; others with different values are seen as a threat. Those centered at Green may tend to be nicer about it, but they will still get the message across when value systems are not in congruence with Green's worldview. All of the levels of 1st Tier will see other values as illegitimate.

The Spiral Dynamics Model says that in general the higher levels on the spiral, such as Orange and Green are growing while the lower levels, Blue and below, are receding in numbers. This is because, in the developed West at least, the living conditions are growing more complex, and people need to think in more complex ways to survive and thrive. Those who stay at their current level when the world around them grows more complex will suffer, because their way of thinking and being is becoming less congruent with the world in which they find themselves. You see a version of this when some people of my own Baby Boomer generation had to learn how to use a new computer or smartphone, and we had to upgrade our own level of complexity of thought to master the new technology and the expanded world that opened as a result.

People centered at Blue value tradition and feel more comfortable when things stay the same – the design of buildings, the language used in worship, and the like. They seek to obey authority and to conform to the community standards. People centered at Orange value personal growth and success. They are often attracted to megachurches and want to add technology and better production values to worship. The contemporary mass in the Catholic Church was made for them. If Jewish, they may move to a reformed temple. Those at Green tend to prefer smaller, more intimate groups with non-traditional ceremonies and are in favor of things like marriage equality. Green is not interested in rules, finances, who makes the most or has the most, competition, buildings, or material goods in general. They are interested in having a fulfilling experience of community in a safe space.

"Nothing stops an organization faster than people who believe that the way you worked yesterday is the best way to work tomorrow."
~ Jon Madonna

When Traditionalist-Blue was the norm for Americans in social settings – up through the 1950's or so, a spiritual leader only needed to open the doors to a place of worship to get attendance. It was what you were supposed to do, so people centered at Blue did it – and still do. As more people evolved to Modernist-Orange, they began to question their faith – both because the theological values presented were often at a different level of cultural evolution, and because it was a beautiful Friday, Saturday, or Sunday, and life was calling! Why shouldn't the stores be open and junior soccer league be held on Sunday mornings?

As people evolve into Postmodernist-Green, they once again seek community, but the Blue level theology is often seen as no longer relevant, and the Orange focus on individual wealth and status is a definite turn-off.

It is much different for a spiritual leader to attract and keep people at the levels beyond Blue. It just is. To add to the challenge, more and more people are evolving along the spiral sooner in life as time goes by. Many millennials have evolved to Orange or Green in their 20's. That is a significant part of the reason the level of Sabbath attendance is plummeting among young people across the developed world.

In my own faith tradition, New Thought, spiritual communities and organizations are usually centered at Orange and/or Green. This is not universal, but it is generally the case. There is insufficient research to show what happens when organizations move from Orange-centered to Green-centered. My observations and study indicate that there is a tendency to shrink in size or at least stop growing, to become more marginal with finances, and to have issues with leadership and decision making as new levels assert themselves. Leaders may have difficulty holding people accountable and enforcing standards of behavior or achievement. It becomes very difficult to fail or to fire someone.

This is consistent with what we know to be the value systems in play at these levels of cultural evolutionary development – as noted earlier, there is a degree of rejection of the previous level that one no longer fully occupies. Many of the larger spiritual communities today are centered at Blue and Orange. Blue focuses on absolute right and wrong and strict adherence to scriptural authority. It provides a stable, well-defined set of rules and standards to live by, as well as clear sets of punishments and rewards.

At Orange, the focus is usually on personal growth and prosperity (remember, Orange is an individualistic level), with some carefully edited focus on scripture in many cases. There are many who straddle the Blue and Orange levels for some time as they make the transition fully from one level to the other. This can be a time for questioning their faith and for great personal and spiritual struggle. They may, for example, maintain a strong Blue value system in their home life, while their working world demands an Orange value system ("Hey, that's business!")

An important value that emerges with Postmodernist-Green is to be strongly egalitarian and therefore anti-hierarchical. At this level, ranks, labels, special privileges, or special recognitions are not valued. This is the level that brought us T-Ball for kids with no score-keeping, so that no child would fell diminished (and to make things less competitive). Everyone is a winner. Nothing should be said or published that might make anyone feel diminished for say, not giving as much money to the spiritual community as someone else. Green is where the concepts of "microaggressions" and "trigger warnings" arose, along with attempts to limit free speech on campuses and other places where offensive things may be spoken.[3] Those at Green genuinely seek a world where everyone feels welcomed and appreciated, but they lack the ability (which develops with 2nd Tier) to see the value in different levels of the spiral than they occupy.

When Green dominates the community culture, Modernist-Orange tends to become frustrated with all the processing and caring about feelings and may even leave the community, while Traditionalist-Blue tends to dig in and fight for the way it used to be. Those at Blue will be on the lookout for any violations of established rules, principles, and guidelines, while speaking often of how good things used to be when "right-thinking" people shared "decent values."

Knowing something about cultural development and values systems gives spiritual leaders insight into the development and the complexity of themselves and the members of their communities; it also gives insight into others with whom the spiritual communities have connections. This insight is valuable, because making everyone else wrong will drive people away.

The Beloved Community at the local level will, naturally, take on the flavor of the dominant value systems present. At Blue, it will likely be leadership driven with mandatory participation. At Orange, it will need to satisfy the individual's desire for personal growth and to be visible in their giving to the cause. At Green, it will most likely be grass-roots driven with flexible communal leadership.

---

[3] This is not the first time in human history where something like "political correctness" has existed; think of fascist regimes, for example. But the value system underlying the Green style of correctness is about ensuring that no one is hurt or offended. That is not the case in such dynamics at lower levels on the spiral.

At 2nd Tier, it may well involve all of these. Once someone becomes centered at Yellow or Turquoise, the entire spiral is valued and attempts are made to include everyone. However, 2nd Tier leadership may face difficulties from some of the 1st Tier levels present, as those in 1st Tier levels will likely see 2nd Tier values as corrupt as well. This requires 2nd Tier leaders to expand their ability to communicate to the value systems present in the community and to speak and listen to them in ways that allow everyone's values to be respected. We will explore this more in the next chapter.

5 THE SPIRAL AND COMMUNITY

"Don't search for heaven and hell in the future.
Both are now present.
Whenever we manage to love
without expectations, calculations, negotiations,
we are indeed in heaven.
Whenever we fight, hate, we are in hell.
~ Shams Tabrizi

The question is – How does *The Beloved Community* arise?

Here, we can look to the spiral – to Spiral Dynamics™ (see Chapter 4) and the emergence and development of complexity and values systems in individuals and groups. *The Beloved Community* is inclusive, but it must also be relational; people must be able to communicate deeply and connect mentally and emotionally. Such connection normally happens more easily when there is homogeneity or *alikeness* present. Diversity often presents some challenges to a group unless and until diversity becomes a valued concept and is extended to become *inclusion* where everyone has a vital and equal seat at the table. We can see this evolution of values systems when we look at diversity along the spiral.

"Diversity ... is not polite accommodation. Instead, diversity is, in action, the sometimes painful awareness that other people, other races, other voices, other habits of mind, have as much integrity of being, as much claim on the world as you do. And I urge you, amid all the differences present to the eye and mind, to reach out to create the bond that will protect us all. We are meant to be here together."
~ William Chase

The levels in the Spiral Dynamics Model are best seen as "containers" for information and ideas. Each level of existence offers a different filtering system of interpretation. The values particular to each level determine how events are interpreted and constitute the worldview of those centered at that level. When a spiritual leader gives a sermon to a group of people who are operating at different levels on the spiral, she is giving a different sermon to each level present.

Diversity is a challenging issue at every level of the 1st Tier, but especially at Traditionalist-Blue and below as there is a basic difficulty with acceptance of someone who is "other." At Tribal-Purple, anyone not identified as a tribe or family member is suspect; at Egotist-Red, everyone beyond the individual is continually suspect and being watched (the world is a jungle filled with dangers).

The absolutist value system at Blue can make openness to people who are different in appearance and/or values challenging. Modernist-Orange is open to diversity but does not necessarily embrace differences; they are just willing to do business with or alongside them. It is at Postmodern-Green where the celebration of diversity becomes a value – and where inclusion begins to be seen as a positive goal. But even at Green (which, remember, is still a fear-based level), there is often a reluctance to accept people who express values different than those of the in-group.

This may appear within Green as an acceptance of the values of anyone who is seen as very different, while being judgmental about differences among the in-group. For example, many at Green want those from immigrant cultures to keep their language and traditions, but they demand that those at Orange and below have the same values regarding diversity and also that they speak in "politically correct" terms.

The concept of equality for LBGTQ people is a very big issue for those at Blue, largely because there is almost always written authoritative sources from an authority saying that to be homosexual or to act upon it is sinful or wrong. Those at Orange may not really care about the issue much, but are open to things like marriage equality from a "live and let live" standpoint; Orange is also happy to make money from LBGTQ consumers. Green will tend to embrace the value of marriage equality and will make those at Blue and below wrong for opposing it.

Different expressions of *The Beloved Community* will, therefore, develop at different levels on the spiral. For groups centered at Blue or below on the spiral, anything resembling *The Beloved Community* will require a high degree of congruence of values and perhaps even appearance. This is the realm of fundamentalism or absolute belief. Outsiders and others who appear to be different will almost always be suspect until they are fully adopted into the community and accepted by authority figures, and even then, there may be lingering suspicions.

In a community centered at Orange, there will be strong support for one another's personal growth, since Orange is an individualistic level (think of the 1980s ME Generation). However, away from the community, the personal life of those at Orange may be very segregated. Remember that those at Orange are interested in status – how they are seen by others – and one way to ensure your own status is to find ways to make others seem "less than" you or your group.

Also, the Orange level of existence is where the concept of relativism enters one's value system in a significant way. Absolutist dogma becomes a turn-off and those at Orange are leading the flight from traditional denominations in the developed world. Orange is the level at which the suburban mega-church or prosperous synagogue is popular, where some conservative spiritual values are acceptable, but it is also acceptable to have wealth and power. As an example, the "Prosperity Gospel" speaks to this level on the spiral.

At Green, *The Beloved Community* might look a bit neo-tribal, as Tribal-Purple values tend to resurface at Green in the love of ritual and in more intimate communal ways of being. A Green-centered group, being egalitarian and emotionally focused, is the most likely to be diverse and to value differences – except for major differences of opinion. Green may also bring crystals and essential oils to the spiritual community and look for New Age books and music in the book store. Or they may seek to study the Kabbalah in a synagogue or explore Sufism in a mosque.

It is the Green level of existence from which the great human and civil rights movements of the past century arose. It is Green calling for the inclusion of LBGTQ community members, women, and people of color in leadership positions of various denominations. Someone centered at Green just may have a problem with you if you do not agree fully with their agenda. However, as noted above, Green will not require that people of other cultures fully adapt to the dominant culture; they will be encouraged to maintain much of their home culture. Also, those at Green will be very concerned with what others are thinking and feeling as they want to understand other people better.

A spiritual community which becomes involved in U.S. immigration issues may see their members who are at Blue being adamant that the laws be enforced absolutely and that all immigrants learn English; those at Orange being willing to work out a pragmatic solution that allows businesses to have workers; and those at Green questioning whether we should even have borders while celebrating those who choose to keep their home language.

It is now common for spiritual communities to be composed of people from several levels on the spiral – Blue, Orange, and Green, perhaps even some at Yellow from the 2nd Tier. To remain sustainable, these communities will need to expand what is acceptable to include the diversity of value systems that come with the presence of multiple levels of existence. The presence of larger degrees of relativism makes it difficult for many traditional denominations and communities to continue to grow and expand as more people embrace relativistic worldviews.

Accommodating the diversity of value systems can be even more challenging than the issue of diversity of appearance because we are not generally aware that such values systems even exist and are valid, much less that they are tied to specific developmental levels on the spiral.

My conclusion is that in the face of such challenges, the best possibility of attaining and maintaining *The Beloved Community* is when enlightened spiritual leadership is present. Such leadership has the awareness of the dynamics present and the competencies to work with people at all levels of the spiral. These competencies include the appropriate measure and use of authority.

Authority will need to be expressed in different ways according to which spiral levels are present. Up until the mid-20th century, what we now call healthy Blue leadership was seen as the ideal. This was usually a man[4], vested with authority by some institution or the founder of an institution. But since the mid-20th century has passed, we are seeing more and more people moving up the spiral into Orange, Green, and beyond. Their view of authority and how one responds to it is significantly different than the traditional values of Blue (although Blue values are still present, they are no longer primary).

Leadership today must include both the awareness and the ability to expand beyond any individual level on the spiral and include other value systems, or the group will tend to center at the level of the leader or the "in-group." This makes creating *The Beloved Community* more difficult, perhaps, but like any other skillset, once it is mastered, it becomes second nature. This is why having a knowledge of the emerging field of cultural evolution is so essential today.

---

[4] With women such as Mary Baker Eddy, the founder of Christian Science, being notable exceptions – and very few and far between.

While those centered at Blue have a strong respect for authority and leadership, those who have moved to Orange generally do not – at least not in the same way. Orange cooperation is not automatic; it must be earned by leadership helping the individual at Orange to get what he seeks. Those at Orange also tend to respect decisive leadership, but not leadership that is locked into inflexible dogma. Those at Orange want to get a divorce when they choose to.

At Green, which, remember, is very egalitarian and anti-hierarchical, the leadership role is more that of a facilitator and coach. Those at Green also have less automatic respect for credentials as signs of authority or expertise. It takes a higher degree of leadership mastery to achieve *The Beloved Community* when you have a mix of levels present. However, in any case, leadership is a very important component of any spiritual community.

"There is almost a sensual longing for communion with others who have a large vision. The immense fulfillment of the friendship between those engaged in furthering the evolution of consciousness has a quality impossible to describe."
~ Pierre Teilhard de Chardin, S.J.

Here, Pierre Teilhard de Chardin speaks to the critical importance of spiritual community in our life. He saw it as a place to be called forward into a great vision - a place where our inner genius and love is allowed, even encouraged, to emerge. This can occur at any level on the spiral, however, where multiple levels are present in the same community, one is better off knowing about cultural evolution and the large role that it plays in human dynamics if one's aim is to facilitate such a harmonious community.

Absent an awareness of the spiral, our natural response to different value systems is to see them as either wrong, ignorant, or corrupt. This leads to disharmony and missed opportunities to learn to coexist and build something wonderful together. Those centered at Green will tend to respond negatively to the authoritarian leadership valued by those at Blue and to the decisive, bottom-line orientation of Orange leadership. Green values cooperation, collaboration, and consensus. These can be seen as cumbersome by Orange and dangerous by Blue.

What is the answer? Perhaps it is 2nd Tier leadership – from the Yellow or Turquoise levels on the spiral.

Integral-Yellow is the first level of 2nd Tier. It is individualistic and very complex. Yellow is a true systems thinker, seeing linkages beyond what most centered in 1st Tier can see. Yellow is also the first level where fear is not the primary driver as it is in all the 1st Tier levels. Think of this fear present in 1st Tier as "if everyone doesn't think the way I or we do, we are all doomed." At Yellow, on the other hand, one sees diversity of thought as a plus.

When one is centered at Yellow, there is little or no energy expended toward ego defense; one has a healthy and high self-concept and does not concern herself with what others think of her. Yellow will engage in vigorous discussions about issues without thinking that she is being personally attacked when someone disagrees. She may disagree with the ideas of others and be surprised when they take it personally. Even when she is personally attacked, her response is likely to be self-examination and either an acceptance of a need to change or a recognition that the attack is not valid. She is not crushed by it nor is she elated by compliments – she holds her own counsel.

Holistic-Turquoise is a communal and very spiritual level of the spiral. Here, a global consciousness truly emerges and one sees that all things are connected in a web of evolving and unfolding energy. The spiritual implications of the Turquoise level are incredibly profound, but a very small percentage of the world population is currently centered here. Also, there are profound differences between the theology of most religions centered at 1st Tier and the kind of spirituality that emerges at Turquoise.

Another distinction to be made regarding Turquoise, and in fact, all the levels, is that of states and stages[5]. A state is a temporary experience of something, such as an experience of oneness or a sense of being out of one's body during a meditative practice. A stage is a more permanent level of existence. So, states of consciousness, such as those experienced in every tradition by saints and sages can occur at any level, or stage, on the spiral. It is important to note that the state experience will be interpreted and given meaning according to the stage occupied by the person having the state experience. Religious or mystical experiences are state experiences; however, they will be understood according to the stage of development of the person having the experience, and observers will understand it according to their own levels of existence. A failure to grasp this distinction can lead to a great deal of confusion and conflict and become a major distraction to the vision and mission of a spiritual community.

---

[5] The work of Ken Wilber, especially in his book *A BRIEF HISTORY OF EVERYTHING* is a good guide for those seeking more on states and stages.

"It's a recognition that reality as we know it is being animated by an evolutionary current. This is true of the cosmological large-scale structure of the universe. It's true biologically. But it's true on a human level, too. The great mystery is living and wanting to transcend itself through us toward greater expressions of beauty, truth, and goodness. And so evolutionary spirituality says that, for lack of a better word, God is implicate, intrinsic to that evolutionary push."
~ Rev. Bruce Sanguin

Only from the 2nd Tier levels can the entire spiral be recognized as consisting of valid values systems. Leaders centered at 1st Tier levels can expand their awareness and their acceptance of difference to a degree, but it does not come naturally; they are in a fear-based level of being. So, we see the additional difficulty in creating *The Beloved Community* when 2nd Tier leadership is absent. It requires enlightened leadership, but enlightened leaders (whether 1st Tier leaders who are very open or 2nd Tier leaders) may not be readily available.

This is a critical area of concern for spiritual organizations and those in such organizations who oversee the education and training of spiritual leaders. While some training and education programs are thorough, very few, if any, currently offer the kind of cultural evolutionary training that is increasingly important today. And very few provide in-depth personal introspection and shadow work in a supportive, professional environment. Many of these training programs are unwittingly setting their students up for failure.

Many things can and will be learned "on the job," but it is unlikely that a working knowledge of cultural evolution is one of them – it is simply not in the standard lexicon in our culture. It is, however, an active element in how people develop, interact, and form community.

The result of this organizational failure to provide an evolutionary approach to education and training programs is a cadre of spiritual leaders who are ill-equipped to understand the cultural evolutionary dynamics unfolding in themselves, their spiritual communities, and the larger society. Additionally, there are many who have not done the personal spiritual and psychological work to help them move beyond the basic fear-based ego needs which hamper the emergence of effective spiritual leadership. At its extremes, this results in abuse; at a minimum, it tends to produce an ineffective spiritual leadership, resulting in spiritual communities which struggle to survive.

I will add a personal caveat here. Those centered at the Postmodern-Green level on the spiral have difficulty with anything approaching rigor or strict standards in education, training, and evaluation. There is a great reluctance at this level to judge the competence or intentions of others, or to subject students to educational processes that make them uncomfortable. This is a growing issue in the larger culture as more and more people move into Green. Enlightened approaches must be found to develop programs and evaluation processes which contain both sufficient rigor and support to better ensure that qualified students achieve success while those who are not well qualified are directed toward pursuits better suited to their abilities.

Spiritual leaders who have not done the kind of personal transformation work described above will have great difficulty in rising above their own ego needs in their leadership roles. I believe this kind of work is necessary for two reasons. First, it allows the person to develop a more authentic level of spiritual maturity resulting in the capacity for true servant leadership and compassion based on spiritual principles; second, it makes the transition to 2nd Tier more likely and perhaps more smooth. Such work also makes for a healthier existence at 1st Tier levels.

"You have to do the work to develop real empathy. There's a cost to evolving: if you want your soul to cross the line, there's no way around emotional work. Face that deep pain, and you gain tremendous compassion for yourself. You feel compassion for those who have hurt you because they were hurt themselves. To really make yourself available to consciously create a new future, you have to do that work."
~ Rev. Bruce Sanguin

The Beloved Community must be a vision-lead group and that vision must be toward the realization and the expression of compassion and love. What is often missing from well-intentioned communities is a large enough number of people who have personally realized a sense of spiritual maturity. Without that realization, the capacity to hold one another in both love and accountability from a healthy perspective is diminished.

Holding others accountable is difficult for those centered at Orange, who are more interested in their own individual issues, or at Green, where hurting the feelings of others is taboo. Those at Blue can do it because the rules are written down and must be obeyed but that only works if the other members of the community are also at Blue, which is becoming increasingly rare as time passes. It has been shown that those centered at 1st Tier

Levels can self-organize and hold one another accountable as a team – see Frederic LaLoux's *REINVENTING ORGANIZATIONS*[6] for examples of this, but these examples are all of organizations with 2nd Tier leadership.

An understanding of the spiral and the cultural evolutionary dynamics that create it gives a spiritual leader essential information about himself and about the people with whom he is interacting. It also provides a greater sense of the overall dynamics of the culture at large – dynamics which affect the spiritual community in a variety of ways.

The Beloved Community arises more quickly and effectively when there is a clear vision, and there are few elements inhibiting its formation and development. These elements can include ineffective leadership, poor interpersonal dynamics, and a lack of coherence between the philosophy of the community and the ways that the philosophy is practiced. Any of these can delay or even halt the development of *The Beloved Community.*

Spiritual leaders must both practice and model effective and compassionate leadership, as well as positive and empathetic interpersonal dynamics. They must display coherence in the presentation and practice of the philosophy and the vision of the spiritual community. That can be a huge challenge, but it is an essential one.

A sound knowledge of cultural evolutionary models gives spiritual leaders a greater potential to create *The Beloved Community* at the local level, which then feeds into the Universal Beloved Community that Dr. Martin Luther King, Jr. envisioned.

---

[6] Laloux, Frederic, *REINVENTING ORGANIZATIONS*, Nelson Parker, 2014

6 PRESENCING

Presencing: To sense, tune in, and act from one's highest future potential—the future that depends on us to bring it into being. Presencing blends the words 'presence' and 'sensing' and works through "seeing from our deepest source."
~ The Presencing Institute

The concept of presencing comes to us from a group that includes Peter Senge, C. Otto Scharmer, Joseph Jaworski, and Betty Sue Flowers in their best-selling leadership book, *PRESENCE*[7]. Written by business people and M.I.T. social scientists, it is also one of the most spiritual books of our age.

I say this because the concepts and practices presented in this book, and in C. Otto Scharmer's later book, *THEORY U*[8], have a

---

[7] Senge, Scharmer, Jaworski, Flowers, *PRESENCE: Human Purpose and the Field of the Future*, Crown Publishers, 2008

[8] Scharmer, C. Otto, *THEORY U: Leading from the Future as it Emerges*, Berrett-Koehler Publishers; 1st Edition (January 1, 2009)

significantly spiritual tone. If you think of presencing as the way you exist energetically, that is, the way you present yourself into the space you occupy and how others experience you, and you see Scharmer and the others are showing how to call that forth from what they call "Source," or a great power that is both beyond and within you, I think you will get my point.

"Energy follows attention. Wherever you place your attention, that is where the energy of the system will go. 'Energy follows attention' means that we need to shift our attention from what we are trying to avoid to what we want to bring into reality."
~ C. Otto Scharmer

Presencing is a key element of creating *The Beloved Community* because it helps us to understand how the spiritual leader is presencing himself to the community and how he can go about improving the quality of how the member's presence to the world.

Imagine how it might feel for someone to enter your spiritual community and encounter the spiritual leader, perhaps yourself, for the first time. What might their experience be? How do you think it would feel? What kinds of sensations would be experienced? What would they take away energetically? Do you have any idea how people experience your community?

If you are a spiritual leader, how do you feel when you encounter a new visitor? What do you see yourself projecting into the space that includes both of you? Is that energy the same or different as when you are with a long-time member? What is your mind doing in such a circumstance? Are you relaxed or anxious, energized or complacent? Are you thinking of what to say, to follow a script for newcomers, or are you more in the moment? Are you sensing anything about the presence of the other person – noticing their uniqueness for example?

I am not speaking about consciously exerting any kind of energy; this isn't about a competitive sense of power nor about ego needs. Presencing is the expression of who you currently are and from what inner depth you are expressing. The shallower the level, the more needy or competitive will be the energy you are presencing. The deeper the level, the more authenticity and compassion will be felt.

If we expand this concept to include the entire spiritual community, what is the experience of being in a space with them? What is the community *presence*? This is something that a spiritual leader may or may not have consciously thought about, but few things are more important as you create *The Beloved Community*. Understanding the energy fields generated by the spiritual leaders in the community is important. Knowing that energy follows attention is invaluable in designing both personal practices and in focusing the leader's communications both inside and outside the spiritual community.

The definition at the beginning of this chapter says that to presence is to sense, tune in to, and act from one's future potential. Becoming aware of our present way of presencing is an important step, but only a first step. We also want to learn to tap into our future potential – to develop a connection to what is ready to emerge from within ourselves and our spiritual communities. Scharmer provides a map to do that in his *Theory U* book.

To develop ourselves so that we naturally presence our best aspects, and so that we continue to develop and grow over time, we must constantly practice the things which help reveal our emerging future. This means that we develop spiritual practices that go deeper toward the level of being where we are no longer driven by ego needs but become the receiver of realization and experience. In other words, we tap into the deepest part of the self and the soul. This deep work is also spiritual in nature, and like most spiritual work, it is not easy.

"What you are, thunders so loud that I cannot hear what you say."
~ Ralph Waldo Emerson

We create our sense of presence over time by the way we express energy when we are with others. If we are highly fear-based and feel the need for strong ego defenses, we express that as a need for attention and, perhaps, an excessive sensitivity, or being "thin-skinned," when we do not get attention or when others dismiss us or disagree with us. While our presence is deeper than our responses, it is the energy that we convey into the room that is perceived by others. How we handle various situations, as well as how we are emotionally when we handle them, will say much to those who surround us about who we are.

Presencing is the dynamic of the giving and receiving of energy in encounters with others, whether one-on-one or in a group. We tend to attract to us those who experience us as congruent with whom they see themselves to be. Others will simply move on.

Those who remain will occupy a spectrum of congruency from positive to negative; some will stay to agree with the spiritual leader, others to do battle. Their motivation is their own, as is the spiritual leader's – and this process will be largely unconscious unless one has done the deep inner work of self-realization over some length of time.

It is said that spiritual community is where people go to work out their childhood issues. While this may be humorous, it is also largely true. However, this is not a negative thing – we always come to spiritual community with something to heal, something to move beyond, to transcend. When the spiritual leader recognizes this and has done his own inner work to a sufficient degree, he can be an effective teacher to the members who show up wounded in ways they may or may not be aware.

There is an art each great spiritual leader has mastered. It is the art of successfully inviting people into a commitment to engage in deep personal transformation. This art arises out of the sense of presence in the leader and who he has become within himself. People are attracted, ideally, because they are inspired by the energy of the leader and desire a similar type of expression for themselves.

So, from where is the spiritual leader expressing herself to the wounded newcomer? If from a place of ego-defensiveness and unhealed wounds, then that newcomer may not be well-served in the spiritual community. On the other hand, the two may engage in a mutual dance of self-discovery and healing as each awakens something new in the other. That is always a possibility in the field of potential outcomes.

How does this work?

I will describe one aspect from the book *Theory U* by Scharmer. It refers to the levels of awareness from which we act or converse. Imagine a large U. As we go down the left side of the U, we deepen our level of awareness; on the right side of the U is the corresponding result, or level of action or discourse that results.

The surface (top of the U) is called "Downloading." Here, the conversation is largely automatic and within the expectations of the participants. Scharmer calls it "speaking from what they want to hear." For example, in your spiritual community, there are ways to speak to one another that become automatic and do not call forth anything deeper than a cursory response. About 95% of our daily conversation exists at this level, including things like greetings, good-byes, perfunctory responses at meetings, when doing commerce, etc.

"Hi, how are you?"

"Hello, I'm fine, thanks, how about you?"

"How about this weather?"

Downloading is everyday behavior that is unlikely to cause anyone to go deep within on any level. The exception would be when everyday speech or action triggers something in someone. Downloading is relatively mindless; you do not speak your mind here, in fact, you hold back so as not to upset anyone. Maybe it's not the time or place, maybe you are just afraid, or maybe Downloading is all that is needed here. Downloading is conforming to the norms of the group and not doing anything unexpected.

The next level down the left side of the U is called "Debate." Debate is "speaking from what I think." This takes the conversation to a deeper level. There will be challenges to the norm and someone may be upset by what is said. An example is when a board member challenges the spiritual leader on an issue where the disagreement may be voiced in the presence of someone who may not be expecting that disagreement. In part, Debate is about disrupting patterned thinking. It is where minds may become receptive to new ideas even with some discomfort.

"Thank you, have a nice day."

"Hey, you gave me the wrong change!"

"What? Really? Let me see."

This example of the Debate level shows the disruption of the normal Downloading pattern that occurs when someone speaks their mind. Such behavior may be frowned upon in some settings, and it may take some degree of courage for someone to speak up and say that the "emperor has no clothes." An example of the Debate level is when someone speaks up and says that a sexist joke is not appreciated. When encouraged and well-managed, Debate can bring new thinking into a group or an organization.

The Debate level can be activated in a positive manner. An example would be when someone reminds us that we need to appreciate the efforts of someone who has worked hard behind the scenes to do something positive. We are called to a deeper level of realization by such comments.

The third level down the left side of the U is called "Dialogue" and is "speaking from seeing myself as a part of the whole." At this level, you are speaking and acting from the viewpoint of someone who is central to what is happening. There is a greater openness and sense of familiarity – of love, if you will.

"Have we looked at how we are being with the new members? Perhaps we are not bringing our best selves forward. I noticed that Mary was upset after the service. Does anyone know what happened?"

"Good point. Let's set aside the next item on the agenda. Tell me more about your sense of this. Let's see what each of us is experiencing regarding this issue."

At this level, my heart, my emotions, are involved. I can change my emotional set point about someone or something. Empathetic listening is now possible – I can feel what the other feels. There are more "we" statements in the conversation. There is license to speak your truth at this level, meaning that there is permission to upset people if that is what speaking your truth does. In return, you agree to come from your most authentic self and endeavor to be kind rather than caustic in any critical statements. The value of this is acknowledged in the group.

Dialogue takes a lot of energy at first, which is the sense of overcoming the automatic restrictions of Downloading and the emotional distance of Debate. Once the group has operated at this level for a time, the energy flows easily and almost effortlessly. You may well feel energized after a board meeting where Dialogue is practiced. There is a release of the need to control, the need to protect oneself. We are all one here. This increases the possibility of a high degree of honesty.

Dialogue comes from the heart; it is an emotionally driven conversation containing the wisdom of the heart. The kindness is not perfunctory; it is genuine. There is a mutual honoring of one another and a willingness to speak your own truth without fear of others taking it personally. There may be the need for clarifying conversations at this level – there must be agreements to be open and receptive to someone else's truth at the Dialogue level.

The deepest level of the U is called "Presencing." Scharmer calls this "speaking from what is moving through." Here, we are operating at great personal depth, completely open – mind, heart, and will – to what he calls Source. The idea of "Leading from an Emerging Future" speaks to the consciousness of operating from the Presencing level.

"Isn't there a way to break the patterns of the past and tune into our highest future possibility—and to begin to operate from that place?"
~ C. Otto Scharmer

At this level, we release our attachments to the past and open to a generative flow from within, you might think of it as accessing your inner intuitive wisdom. There is a release of will – the most difficult thing to release – resulting in a complete openness to what emerges.

The Presencing level can be reached individually or in a group. Doing so usually involves some type of meditative process. When a leadership team can access this level regularly, there is a great increase in the energy of the entire community. Scharmer says you can tell that you have been at the Presencing level because you emerge a different person.

This level of personal depth can be uncomfortable, even frightening for some. Others may find it difficult to let go of the ego's hold on the mind and to allow them to be open to deeper inner revelations. Spiritual Leaders must first develop their own capacities to do this personally and then be patient with others as they learn this skill.

Each of the deeper levels on the U leads to greater clarity and a greater range of the potential being explored. Succeeding levels create more openness – mind, heart, and will – to different ideas, ways of being, people, and ways of doing things. The deeper you go, the greater the effect.

While there is no need to go beyond Downloading in much of our day-to-day conversation, such as making a purchase at a store, it is advisable to add to your Downloading practices some uplifting comments. Using praise and appreciation in everyday conversation and making the effort to connect with people are good ways to improve the quality of your Downloading level conversations, and it may lead to some unexpectedly deep connections with others.

Accessing the deeper levels of the U can become part of a spiritual leader's personal spiritual practices, and it can be incorporated into group spiritual practices to open meetings, classes, and other activities where a greater sense of presencing would be optimal.

I would often encourage a practice in various meetings of taking a moment of silence during or after each piece of business (such as before and/or after voting on a motion in a board meeting) and suggesting that each person sees how they feel about what just occurred. Is there anything unresolved that still needs to be addressed? Are we ready to move to the next item, being complete with the last? Do we need to take the matter to a deeper level?

Developing a more compassionate and loving presence as a spiritual leader will have a positive effect on every aspect of your work, from sermons and teaching classes, to performing rituals and sacraments, to counseling.

For the spiritual leader, having both a greater awareness of these levels and how they operate and doing regular practice to deepen one's own experience with them will generate a deeper and more compassionate presence as an individual. Expressing greater love, greater compassion, a greater sense of self-confidence, empathy, and more. This is what people seek in a spiritual leader. This is also what enables the spiritual leader to fulfill his role in a more loving and compassionate manner - to be the authentic light that serves the spiritual community from a place of deep integrity.

How we *presence* ourselves has a powerful effect on how we create *The Beloved Community*.

7 EVOLVING LEADERSHIP

"Man who waits for roast duck to fly into mouth must wait very, very long time."
~ Chinese Proverb

In the earlier chapter on leadership (Chapter 3), I wrote about several qualities that are necessary for spiritual leaders to create the kind of organizational environment in which *The Beloved Community* can develop. How do leaders and future leaders identify those qualities and develop them? I am sharing these ideas with you because I found them helpful in my own development as a spiritual leader.

There is a new field of study has emerged containing many important ideas and models for leadership. The field can generally be described as the field of multiple intelligences. It began to develop in the latter third of the 20th century when additional intelligences beyond cognitive intelligence (IQ) began to be mapped and studied. Out of this work, four overall areas of intelligences help us to recognize the importance of understanding multiple intelligences and how to develop ways to enhance our own intelligence and skills.

The four areas are: Physical Intelligence (PQ), Cognitive Intelligence (IQ), Emotional Intelligence (EQ), and Spiritual Intelligence (SQ). Each of these uses different parts of the brain and central nervous system. Of special interest in this chapter are the last two, EQ and SQ.

EQ as we understand it today comes primarily from the work of Daniel Goleman and Richard Boyatsis[9] whose groundbreaking work beginning in the 1980's and 1990's helped us to identify what emotional intelligence is and how we can develop it to higher levels. This is critically important for leadership, as many, if not most of the issues regarding individual leaders can be attributed to a lack of sufficient emotional intelligence.

The definition of EQ: *"Emotional intelligence is the ability to perceive emotions, to access and generate emotions so as to assist thought, to understand emotions and emotional knowledge, and to reflectively regulate emotions so as to promote emotional and intellectual growth."*

EQ is the capacity to manage your own emotional state to such a degree that you are in dominion over your emotional reactions and able to recognize and work effectively with the emotional states of others. Every spiritual leader has had experience with this – dealing with those in crisis or in mourning, for example, or with an angry member. When a spiritual leader is unable to take dominion over his own emotions, he may well say or do something harmful or destructive and deny those with whom he is working the spiritual example that they are rightfully seeking. Daniel Goleman describes five areas of EQ[10]:

1. Self-Awareness: having an awareness of your own emotional states, moods, motivations, etc. Anyone doing deep spiritual practices can develop greater self-awareness and learn to tune in to what is going on within.

---

[9] Emotional Intelligence, as a psychological theory, was developed by Peter Salovey and John Mayer.

[10] *EMOTIONAL INTELLIGENCE*, by Daniel Goleman, Bantam Books; 10th Anniversary Edition (September 27, 2005)

2. Self-Regulation: is the ability to control and direct your emotions so your actions are congruent with the situation that you are facing. Also, in this area are proactive tendencies like high self-regard and open mindedness.
3. Internal Motivation: this refers to having a strong internal compass that directs you toward big goals and values; not money and power, but the ability to affect your world in a positive manner; to see yourself as a contributor of good.
4. Empathy: the ability to understand the emotional states of others; either cognitive empathy – to intellectually understand them based on sensory cues, or emotional empathy – to feel what others are feeling. Empathy is an essential building block for the development of true compassion – of seeing and feeling yourself as one with others.
5. Social Skills: this refers to the ability to effectively manage relationships, build networks, and be at ease with others. It is not manipulative; the management is more of your own emotional self and behaviors. One can be in introvert or extrovert and have good social skills.

From this basic information about EQ, can you see its importance in the development of spiritual leadership? It is my suggestion that everyone study EQ, as it is an essential part of any leadership curriculum including ongoing education, and that it must be included in counseling practices of all kinds. EQ is the key to a great number of dysfunctional behavior in human beings.

Spiritual leaders who stay composed, keep the important things in mind, remember the value of all people, and are big-picture oriented have high EQ. Low EQ often shows up as inappropriate behaviors such as outbursts, gossiping, being "thin-skinned," temper tantrums, and the like. EQ is not just "being nice," it is being centered in a sense of authentic inner authority.

"Emotional intelligence does not mean merely 'being nice.' At strategic moments it may demand not 'being nice,' but rather, for example, bluntly confronting someone with an uncomfortable but consequential truth they've been avoiding."
— *Daniel Goleman*

Many of the people with whom spiritual leaders are called upon to counsel have low EQ. They have not learned to manage their emotions or to have a positive self-concept, and they get into various kinds of difficulty as a result. If the spiritual leader who counsels people with such issues has not developed her own EQ sufficiently, the counseling process is likely to do more harm than good. There are serious consequences when spiritual leaders have low EQ.

Spiritual Intelligence or SQ is a more recently developed concept, and it builds on the work done in EQ. SQ evolved out of the work of people such as Jody Fry, Ph.D., and, especially, Cindy Wigglesworth, who developed the SQ21 Spiritual Intelligence Assessment and Coaching Process[11] [12]. Their work is of immense importance and should be part of the initial and lifelong training of spiritual leaders.

SQ is defined by Wigglesworth as: *Spiritual Intelligence is the ability to behave with wisdom and compassion, while maintaining inner and outer peace, regardless of the situation.*

When we think of great spiritual leaders, regardless of their faith tradition, isn't this what they exemplified? To behave with wisdom and compassion with inner and outer peace, regardless of the situation is an excellent way of describing spiritual maturity.

---

[11] SQ21: The Twenty-One Skills of Spiritual Intelligence, by Cindy Wigglesworth, SelectBooks, Inc.; 1 edition (October 4, 2012)

[12] See also DeepChange.com for more on the assessment and coaching process.

"I have researched 21 measurable 'skills' or 'competencies' that are components of this ability. These include things like 'awareness of one's own worldview,' 'complexity of inner thought,' 'awareness of interconnectedness of life,' 'keeping your Higher Self in charge,' and 'being a wise and effective change agent.' Unlike many spiritual teachings, which can tend to seem vague or mysterious, these tangible skills can be learned through practice and developed through clearly-defined levels."[13]
~ Cindy Wigglesworth

The 21 levels refer to important areas of self-development and social development essential to personal and spiritual growth. As a spiritual leader, one is expected to have done his inner work, and such work is essential to the development of EQ and SQ. In turn, high levels of EQ and SQ are essential to being an effective, aware, compassionate, and competent leader.

The essence of SQ is the development of our capacity to behave with wisdom and compassion regardless of the situation or at a minimum, to do this better than one currently does. SQ and EQ are guides to a greater sense of poise and equanimity.

This does not mean that good spiritual leaders never lose their temper (remember Jesus with the moneylenders), nor that they are never overcome by sadness or loss. It does mean that the level of debilitation is less, and the recovery process from such instances is quicker and more smooth. And it means that it takes more to disturb one to such a degree than it may have in the past.

---

[13] *Huffington Post*, "The Blog," August 10, 2012

"There is a loneliness in us that hears. When the soul parts from the company of the ego and its retinue of petty conceits; when we cease to exploit all things but instead pray the world's cry, the world's sigh, our loneliness may hear the living grace beyond all power."
~ Rabbi Heschel

Spiritual leaders cannot function properly and honor their high calling if they have not developed their emotional and spiritual intelligence to a sufficient degree. If they have not done the work necessary to remain poised when crises arise, when people are upset and angry, when their community members present the same issues that the leader suffers with, when the world around them seems to be losing its bearings, then they will not be available when they are most needed. It is as simple as that.

The Beloved Community will not arise in a house where emotional and spiritual intelligence is low, where too much energy goes into protecting the fragile ego of the spiritual leader, or in cases where the spiritual leader is an active participant in dysfunction. Leaders must lead from a place of credibility and integrity. This does not mean that leaders never make mistakes or they cannot show their vulnerability. It does mean that spiritual leaders must be consciously working to deepen their self-knowledge, EQ and SQ on an ongoing basis.

In fact, the ability to admit mistakes and to show vulnerability is a healthy aspect of integral spiritual leadership; it is also a hallmark of 2nd Tier leadership in the Spiral Dynamics model.

Building on these concepts is the idea of *resonant leadership*, an extension of the EQ work. Richard Boyatsis and Annie McKee have written a book about this idea[14]. Resonant leadership is concerned with humanizing leadership and using practices which encourage mindfulness, compassion, and hope into the realm of leadership. The resonant leader operates with a powerful connection with and resonance to the vision and the people of the spiritual community.

These models and concepts show the evolution of leadership over the past half-century or so. It has gone from a strict, authoritarian model through various ideas of personal empowerment, to a humanizing and personal set of practices.

In Spiral Dynamics terms, it has gone from Traditionalist-Blue through Modernist-Orange to Postmodernist-Green and is beginning to move toward the 2nd Tier levels. In my view, spiritual leadership practices should be at the forefront in this evolutionary process, if for no other reason than because leadership in general is becoming more compassionate, which is in perfect alignment with being more spiritually realized.

In a rapidly changing world, people look to religion and spirituality for comfort and for principles that are not subject to the whims of cultural change. They look for grounding, but not smothering. They seek to know how to live successfully in the world outside the doors of their house of worship but not succumb to the secular principles of that world.

Evolved spiritual leadership can provide what people are looking for, regardless of the faith tradition involved. Spiritual leaders who recognize the importance of psychological transformation as

---

[14] *RESONANT LEADERSHIP: Renewing Yourself and Connecting with Others Through Mindfulness, Hope, and Compassion*, by Richard Boyatsis and Annie McKee, Harvard Business Review Press; 1st Edition (2005)

the vehicle to a more realized spirituality are going to be more effective in guiding people along the spiritual pathway. They help to create a resonant field of connection, of possibility, of love, and of compassion in their own spiritual communities. They empower their members to go into the larger world grounded in spiritual love and capable of thriving in positive ways. They help to develop the compassionate heart and take it out into the world.

The importance of competent, emotionally mature leadership in spiritual community cannot be overemphasized. Underdeveloped leaders easily become a drain on the spiritual community, as their own unmet needs become the focus. Rather than serving, they need to be served.

In exploring the creation of *The Beloved Community* at the local level, I have provided information on several concepts and models for spiritual leaders who desire to gain a foothold in understanding our rapidly changing times.

- Spiral Dynamics™ Model
- Theory U™ & Presencing Models
- Multiple Intelligences
- Emotional Intelligence (EQ)
- Spiritual Intelligence & SQ21™Assessment
- Resonant Leadership

My purpose in presenting these in introductory form is to give spiritual leaders, who may not have thought in an evolutionary way, resources to address many of the challenges that they have been facing – and will continue to face as time goes on. A lack of awareness and understanding of the dynamics of cultural evolution is a significant blind spot shared by all too many spiritual and secular leaders today. It is one that can be eliminated by studying the subject matter and applying it in your spiritual community.

Oh, and evolved spiritual leaders take the long view:

"Nothing that is worth doing can be achieved in our lifetime; therefore, we must be saved by hope. ... Nothing we do, however virtuous, can be accomplished alone; therefore, we are saved by love. No virtuous act is quite as virtuous from the standpoint of our friend or foe as it is from our standpoint. Therefore, we must be saved by the final form of love, which is forgiveness."
~ Reinhold Niebuhr

My hope is that you will explore more about these topics on your own and encourage those on your leadership teams, in your spiritual organizations, and those involved with the education and training of the future spiritual leaders of your organizations to look at them as well. New ideas need champions. Be a champion.

"Don't ask what the world needs. Ask what makes you come alive, and go do it. Because what the world needs is people who have come alive."
~ Howard Thurman

8 SAFE SPACE

"If we want to create spaces that are safe for the soul, we need to understand why the soul so rarely shows up in everyday life."
~ Parker Palmer

A key element in *The Beloved Community* is the concept of safe space. It is also frequently misunderstood. Safe space is sometimes construed as being free from anything that one might find uncomfortable; free from anything that might trigger negative emotions or fear.

Safe space in a spiritual context is something very different. When seen from a spiritual perspective, safe space is a place where you can experience the challenges and dangers of deep and profound spiritual and psychological transformation while surrounded by a supportive environment.

Not everyone is ready to explore deeply when they arrive in spiritual community. Some arrive with fresh wounds, or deep older wounds that have not healed. These folks need a different version of safe space; they need space to heal. Bruce Sanguin speaks of the need for spiritual community to have the capacity to both "envelop" and "develop" its members.

To *envelop* means to surround those who are wounded or traumatized with loving support until they reach a place where they can function well. To *develop* means to assist those who are in a place of stability to move through processes of evolutionary spiritual development with all its potential for pain and difficulty so that they can go to the next level of growth. Spiritual communities need to encompass both enveloping and developing in order for the community itself to be healthy enough to create *The Beloved Community*.

When a spiritual community moves into enveloping full time, the healthier people will tend to leave, as their needs are not being met. If developing is the only focus, those who show up for healing or become wounded may depart because their needs are not being met. It is the conscious expansion of the community's energies into both realms of service that is calling us forth. The blending of the two functions is essential.

A part of the enveloping ministry is to recognize when someone has serious emotional or psychological issues which are beyond the counseling qualifications of those who do spiritual counseling in the spiritual community. Naturally, such people will be prayed for and with, but there should also be a clear policy to refer them to professional mental health practitioners when appropriate. Such people can be a danger to themselves and others, and even the most well-meaning attempts to help them may cause harm.

Spiritual leaders must be versed in such issues and take the proper action should such situations arise.

For us to be fully in spiritual community means spending a lot of time alone in spiritual practices and exploration. If our only spiritual activities occur when we are with the community, we will have little to give, as our personal development will be limited. Personal practice builds the spiritual "muscle" necessary to be a contributor to the energy of love and compassion needed for the creation of *The Beloved Community*.

Safe space in spiritual community is not about eliminating discomfort – it is providing a supportive place where we can experience the inevitable discomfort of deep personal introspection and spiritual growth with support and understanding. Those who seek to eliminate any sense of discomfort for those in their community are, in effect, becoming roadblocks to spiritual growth. This is a very hard lesson for many to learn, particularly those leaders centered at the Green level of development on the spiral.

"The invitation to accept the diamond of life is not an invitation to safety and comfort. It is an invitation to live life fully and completely, which is never safe and is often uncomfortable. . .'If I am safe enough, then I can relax.' I am talking about recognizing that you can relax right now, even though you aren't completely safe and you never will be."
~ Gangaji

Safe space means that we co-create a chrysalis of support for those who are wounded as well as for those who choose to do the deep and often painful work of personal transformation. To suggest that it can be otherwise is misleading. When spiritual community tries to eliminate discomfort, it becomes a place of refuge from the world rather than a point of entry, or perhaps re-entry, *into* the world. The community's mission is effectively turned upside down.

The Beloved Community is centered on expressing deeply embodied spiritual principles into the world around us; it is not about withdrawal or shutting ourselves away. It is never pretending or engaging in spiritual bypass. It is always engaging life in the most authentic manner possible.

A spiritual community wishing to offer truly effective safe space must contain enough spiritually mature and psychologically healthy people to model and teach a healthy spiritual maturity to those who seek it. This means that people will move through stages of discomfort and even pain, because there is no change process in which some degree of discomfort is not a part. Safe space provides a container for transformation. One still goes through the pain and discomfort, but one knows that they are being held in that container.

"Some are born virtuous, some become virtuous. To be good by nature is indeed fortunate but to become good is like walking on a double-edged sword; it takes a longer time and is more painful."
~ Umera Ahmed

A critical element of safe space is provided by the community's spiritual leadership. They create an environment with the capacity to allow people to be themselves, to grow at their own rate, and to speak their truth. This may result in some breaks in decorum, that is, there may be a few occasions where people act out in ways that others find disturbing or offensive. Effective spiritual leadership not only expects such incidents to occur, but uses them as teaching moments for themselves and for the members.

Ideally, the spiritual leader has lived the kinds of experiences that the members of the community experience as they develop spiritually. She has done (and continues to do) the work of personal transformation, felt the fear, the pain, and the longing as the process unfolded. As a result, she has a great compassion for those who are having their own experience – however, that compassion does not include trying to relieve them of the difficulties on their own pathway. Rather, she works to guide them through the process of finding their own way on the path.

This honoring and recognition of the various processes that we all go through empowers the entire spiritual community as members learn and grow. There is no need to feel diminished or less than others because one experiences a "bump" on the road toward spiritual realization. Everyone in the community can feel a sense of empowerment and authenticity when sound spiritual leadership is present. The struggle of the growing process can be recognized, honored, and even celebrated.

"An often overlooked character trait is when you create a level of comfort that allows people to feel safe being themselves around you."
~ Bryan Petersen

The Beloved Community and the notion of safe space are foundational elements in the developing the capacity to handle difficult ideas, experiences, and realities from a position of strength and confidence. If our overall mission in the local spiritual community is to develop and empower people to assist in the creation of the *Universal Beloved Community*, then they will need to be thoroughly grounded in spiritual realization and psychological health. Safe space includes the need to come to terms with the harsh and often difficult realities of being human. In safe space, we are not protected from disturbance, rather we are disturbed in a protected space.

"The Gospel is a very dangerous idea. We have to see how much of that dangerous idea we can perform in our own lives. There is nothing innocuous or safe about the Gospel. Jesus did not get crucified because he was a nice man."
~ Walter Brueggemann

If we are to fulfill our inner urge to live fully as spiritual beings who fully engage life, then we will need to submit ourselves to the challenges of becoming what we envision. Having a safe space in which to practice as we learn and grow is essential, and spiritual community can and does provide just that when it is healthy, functional, and led by spiritually-aware beings. The Beloved Community requires no less.

9 PRESERVING THE MYSTICAL

"The mystical is not the ethical. The former arises from the death or temporary disappearance of the ego; the latter emerges from the affirmation of the ego among many other egos, that is, from an uncompromising privileging of the human person within a community of persons. The mystical cannot lead to the ethical without considerable help from outside and elsewhere, that is, from reason, political theory, moral debate, and a love of human beings, not as ciphers for grand metaphysical realities ("Christ," Brahman," "emptiness," or whatever), but as human beings in all their mundane and messy glory."
~ Jeffrey Kripal, Roads of Excess, Palaces of Wisdom

As I see it, there are two main reasons to be in spiritual community. One is to develop a culture of love and support for people living their daily lives based on spiritual understanding; the other is to introduce them to the mystical path. Each faith tradition may view mysticism differently, but all have a way of understanding and relating to the mystical aspects of life. *The Beloved Community* is made stronger through an awareness and ideally an experience of the mystical. It is where the true meaning of being human resides.

We are taught both how to live in the physical world and how to live in the realms beyond that world in spiritual community. Ideally, both concepts are clarified and "braided together" through spiritual instruction and by example, so that members of the community realize that they literally have a foot in each. From that awareness and understanding, we learn to view our life experiences from a deeper place and to see connections where none were apparent before. We also come to realize that there is more for us to call upon in troubled times than our own understanding of reality.

Philosopher Ken Wilber calls these two functions "translation" and "transformation." *Translation* is the process of learning to view the world through the prism of a new philosophy. It includes new terms, meanings, practices, rituals, and ways of living that are prescribed by each faith tradition. Translation is the process of becoming a member of the culture of a faith tradition. This may take a great deal of time, study, and effort, and it requires significant resources from the spiritual community to provide access to this process. In fact, some never go farther than translation in their spiritual community – it becomes all about living according to certain rules and using certain vocabulary or dressing in accord with some customs, and the concept of personal transformation is delayed or set aside entirely.

Every spiritual community will have translation as an element of being a part of the community. There will be terms, ideas, and behaviors that are either ritualized or have become part of daily practice.

"While it is a necessary function of translational religion to break down the teachings into understandable chunks so that they can be chewed, swallowed and digested, thereby giving coherency and meaning to our lives, we need to remain open to the transformational possibilities inherent in the insecurity, confusion, paradox, the 'beginner's mind,' the ways of not-knowing."
~ Regina Sarah Ryan, PRAYING DANGEROUSLY

Transformation is just what is says – a profound change. Transformation involves change at depth within the individual. It is the process of going beyond learning about one's spiritual nature and actually experiencing it. While there are variations on the processes involved in different faith traditions, they are all pointing toward an awakening of the mystic or the "spiritual self" within each person.

"Nobody has yet invented a Spiritual Calculus, in terms of which we may talk coherently about the divine Ground and of the world conceived as its manifestation."
~ Aldous Huxley, THE PERENNIAL PHILOSOPHY

A mystic is primarily centered within, in the inner life. A mystic is a person who has mastered, or is in the process of mastering, the realization of the inner power of consciousness. The mystic basically turns away from the outer life as the main arena of action; he turns away from depending upon society at the level of ordinary interactions. There are many names for this inner realm and the powers that reside there. One way to look at it is to cultivate one's intuitive nature, the way of knowing that is beyond the five senses. Some call this the Holy Spirit or the Divine Ground, others the collective unconscious. Whatever it is called, it is an aspect of the mystical realm.

Joseph Campbell is a good source for understanding mystical traditions, because he studied so many as a mythologist – studying myths of the world, most in their native languages. The mystical is about interiority, not the external. The external can only represent the mystical through symbolism, as much religious ritual, art, and practice does; it cannot reproduce it. So how is the realized mystic, the one who is aware of her inner identity and in touch with it, to behave?

"You wear the outer garment of the law, behave as everyone else and wear the inner garment of the mystic way. Jesus also said that when you pray, you should go into your own room and close the door. When you go out, brush your hair. Don't let them know. Otherwise, you'll be a kook, something phony."
~ Joseph Campbell

The mystics among us are often not known as such to others. Many, if not most of the saints of various traditions have been mystics, some very openly, others very quietly. A saying in the medieval Christian churches of Europe was, "woe be the bishop who has a saint in his parish." The mystics will see a greater truth and yet may appear insane to those who are grounded in sensory reality. At a minimum, a saint will remind the spiritual leader about where he (the leader) is falling short of living up to his avowed spiritual principles. It is a conundrum in some spiritual communities. My response is — we all should have such a problem as to have a true mystic in our midst.

The richness of mystical experience, especially when taught in community, brings a joy to living, a richness and a depth, that is simply impossible for those who do not get a sense of the mystical in their lives. Spiritual practices of various kinds can lead people closer to the mystical elements within. Many spiritual and religious traditions design their practices and rituals to help members to experience a deeper sense of the mystical. For some, it is the sole focus of spiritual practice.

"When the scientists finally reach the mountain tops of understanding, they will find the mystics waiting for them."
~ Ernest Holmes

We all seek meaning in life, a meaning that is not fully revealed in our day to day lives but in a deeper sense of connection and love that we all share. Every religion has had mystical elements and teachings, and there is a reason for this — without a mystical sense, spirituality and religion become flat, dull, and lifeless.

This is why so many who seek a rich material lifestyle become so frustrated with the emptiness that often results. The soul is not fed by things, or by status, or by celebrity. The soul is fed by meaning, fulfillment, and connection. The soul is fed by the joy of experiencing the mystical side of life with its rich sense of connection to everyone and everything. The soul is fed by the joys and the sorrows of the fully lived human life.

"This is an essential experience of any mystical realization. You die to your flesh and are born into your spirit. You identify yourself with the consciousness and life of which your body is but the vehicle. You die to the vehicle and become identified in your consciousness with that of which the vehicle is but the carrier. That is the God."
~ Joseph Campbell

The death of the body is symbolically represented in many sacraments and practices across the religious spectrum. It is bodily death that the realized mystic seeks – to fully merge with the divine, to shed this mortal coil, and to realize the divine presence as we move away from dependence on just the five senses, and toward a richer inner life.

In modern times, we have our scientific knowledge and other forms of analytical thought to contend with – they are no less real than the mystical, but they can become an obstruction for those on the pathway. The tendency to overthink and to overdevelop the thought processes restricts our access to deeper intuitive knowing, which requires an ability to quiet the analytical mind. The symbolic value contained within mysticism brings a greater sense of aliveness to everyday life.

The Beloved Community is a place where there is a balance between the everyday and the mystical, where both are taught and seen as two elements of a greater whole. Each is accessible, but all must follow the prescribed pathways. The full nature of the mystical realm is infinite, so no human can ever be fully realized as a mystic – there is always more to realize. The possibility for spiritual growth never goes away.

"If Jesus is God, and his Father is God also, what then is the relationship? Jesus said, 'I and my Father are one,' and those words brought him to the cross. Sufi mystic al-Hallaj said the same thing, 'I and my Beloved are one,' and he too was crucified. This is the mystic realization: you and that divine immortal being of beings of which you are a particle, are one. The classical statement of the idea is 'tat tvam asi,' 'you are that,' and the famous formula in the Chāndogya Upanishad: 'you are yourself the divine mystery you wish to know.' 'I and my father are one.'"
~ Joseph Campbell

The crucifixion of Jesus, for the one who understands the mystical connection, symbolizes the fear-based nature of everyday life. Finding the pathway from that fear to a deeper mystical knowing, where fear fades away, is an important aspect of the spiritual pathway. At its highest level, *The Beloved Community* functions from this knowing.

Therefore, the spiritual leader must do her work to realize her own mystical nature and to blend the two natures into a way of being that is effective in both realms. She must do more than create a translational environment in the spiritual community, she must also facilitate an environment where transformation is modeled and encouraged.

"A man who seeks enlightenment should seek it as a man whose hair is on fire seeks a pond."
~ Sri Ramakrishna

The realization of oneness, of enlightenment, of our deep mystical nature, is no less dangerous today than it was in the times of the ancients – the danger is often from the analytical mind, which operates from the fear that one is becoming something that the fear-based ego cannot manage or control. This mind can be seen in ecclesiastical authorities who are stuck in the translational aspect of their religion and who refuse to engage with transformation (beyond lip-service). The fear of self-annihilation is always present on the spiritual pathway. It is our fear of death that can lead us to self-destructive behaviors when we are out of balance.

Where is the list of things to do or to know about the mystical?

Well, there is no one thing. The approach to the mystical life is prescribed in each faith tradition and each may follow it differently. Along the path there are few tangible markers of note – the experience of the mystical may occur at any moment, last for a few seconds, or for many years, and dissolve into nothingness without warning.

"The whole secret of mysticism is this: that man can understand everything by the help of what he does not understand. The morbid logician seeks to make everything lucid and succeeds in making everything mysterious. The mystic allows one thing to be mysterious, and everything else becomes lucid."
~ G.K Chesterton

There are no tangible lessons to be given here, only an idea of the existence of such realms and the importance of living from both the sensory and the mystical can be conveyed. For some, the idea of the mystical may remain unrealized in their personal experience, but that does not make the mystical any less real.

We dance between worlds. We have our analytical capacities which are well-suited to the physical realm but are inadequate to fully explain even the visible structure of reality. The study of quantum physics and related fields has shown us that even the purely physical world is beyond easy understanding; it is beyond the capacity of our sensory apparatus and its analytical extensions to fully comprehend it. It seems that all of reality is beyond our grasp and we must learn to live in the mystery. The mystical realm is the realm of mystery. Even when experienced, it often defies description and analysis.

The mystical realm that transcends and includes the physical is impossible to understand from a sensory-analytical standpoint. Those who have had experiences of the mystical all say that it cannot be described using language. It is more a "beingness" than a "doingness" – and we are only good at describing the doing aspects of our nature.

Mysticism sounds crazy. And it is, from the worldview of the analytical mind, bound as that mind is by what the senses tell it. But there is more to being human than what we can experience through our senses. We can access realms of beingness that allow us to express so much more fully in life. We can become fully actualized human beings, and we can transform the world.

Our spiritual nature is an aspect of the mystical. It has no physical aspect, so it cannot be seen or measured. It is beyond our ability to know, based on the way our brain/mind evolves and is conditioned. But the mystical is as real as anything that we experience in the physical – perhaps more real. And one of the main purposes of spiritual community is to help its members cultivate a deeper relationship with their mystical natures.

"Out there, beyond right-doing and wrong-doing, there is a field.

I will meet you there.

When the soul lies down in that grass, the world is too full to talk about.
Ideas, language - even the phrase 'each other' -
do not make any sense."

~ Rumi

Learning about our mystical nature includes the ego-deflating processes of learning to surrender to something that cannot be fully understood. We are taught to be the masters of our world – to conquer nature and human relationships, to seek fame and fortune – all of which require a belief that all of the necessary knowledge can be known. Then we discover the mystical, which cannot be known, cannot be mastered, and cannot be conquered. It is a realm of mystery that cannot be fully understood; it can only be experienced. We are left to discover the meaning of all of this for ourselves. The introduction to the mystical presages a massive transformation in each person's relationship to our physical and spiritual ways of being.

"Mysticism is the redemption of our consciousness from the lower, partial levels of life by a conscious, personal recognition of its high levels which are open and available to all who seek their blessings."
~ W.L. Barth

The old joke goes: *"How do I get to Carnegie Hall?"* The answer: *"Practice."*

"How do I get to access the mystical realm?" "Do your practices regularly."

Of all the spiritual practices available, meditation is the most effective for this purpose. While one cannot control the mystical realm, one can invite it into awareness through the silence and solitude of meditation. This is the one way that has been demonstrated to be effective. Long term meditation practices serve to train the mind how to quiet the tendency to overthink, quieting the "monkey mind," to invite the deeper wisdom to rise into conscious awareness. There is something that you can do; you can do your spiritual practices.

There are several connections between the mystical aspects of religious philosophy and the development of *The Beloved Community*. One is an expanded view of reality that comes from the development of one's mystical side. From the deep practices that lead us toward a greater realization of the mystical, we expand and deepen our awareness of the potentialities that we possess on the physical side. This includes a greater capacity for compassion and love arising from a greater sense of connection. There is often a reduction in fear within us. As we leave behind the idea that separation is a part of our reality (which is what our senses tell us about the physical realm), a new sense of connection emerges within us.

When we recognize the value of stillness, of activities like meditation and contemplation on our lives we are spiritually expanded. When we plumb the depths of our being in spiritual practice, we are deepened. When we are expanded and deepened, a greater, more loving, more powerful version of ourselves emerges. From this emergence, the reality of *The Beloved Community* is strengthened. From that place of awareness and realization, we are ready to serve the larger world from an authentic sense of contribution.

"I told my students that this was the time to learn that stillness does not mean silence. It means being still, sitting down in the midst of it all, allowing everything to happen just as it is happening, being willing to listen and see and sense without clinging or contracting and pushing away. I told them that meditation is an act of non-resistance. It is the act of being still, grounding ourselves in the body and the breath, coming down out of our heads and touching the earth again, being willing to bear witness to what arises, all the things that need to be heard and seen and felt, inside and outside."
~ Tracy Cochran

10 COMMUNITY IN ACTION

"Never forget that social justice is what love looks like in public"
~ Cornel West

Community in action touches on the essential nature of spiritual community. It refers to the healthy and loving pursuit of the consciousness of compassion and mutual expression of love necessary to manifest *The Beloved Community*, and to LIVE that heartfully in the world. I believe regardless of the form that a spiritual community takes, the creation of *The Beloved Community* can be a major reason for its being. And I believe that *The Beloved Community* can be created regardless of the form that a spiritual community takes.

There are as many forms of spiritual community as there are faith traditions, and within each faith tradition, sub-forms emerge so that no two individual spiritual communities are exactly alike. Some are primarily focused inward, effectively shutting out the outer world to one extent or another. Others are primarily outwardly focused, which usually means the focus is on trying to convert others to the faith tradition of that community. Some are primarily about *translation* (see Chapter 9); others extend toward *transformation*.

But there is, if you will, a larger way of being in spiritual community, especially if the desire is to create an authentic version of *The Beloved Community*. We can think of this as a both/and position – a strong inward focus on the spiritual principles of the faith tradition which then enables members of the community to engage the larger world from the position of having embodied those principles.

Here the aim is not to convert but to selflessly serve the larger community. Nothing is sold or marketed, there is no agenda beyond service, and there is simply a natural expression of compassion and love that has arisen in people who have learned and are practicing deep spiritual principles. Being a part of such a community ignites the desire to be of service in whatever forms the larger community needs at any given moment.

In evolutionary terms, the emergence of a transformational community of practice and realization becomes a strong attractor to those who seek to connect with such an energy. Like attracts like.

"As we grow in our commitment to racial equality or social justice, we have to be very imaginative. We have to find ways that have transformative potential."

~ Walter Brueggemann

The Beloved Community expresses in many ways. It can be through formalized outreach programs or everyday interactions with people. It can be in group activities or by individuals expressing embodied spiritual principles inside or outside the spiritual community. It can be members of a contemplative community who never leave their property and who commit their lives to spiritual practices. There are many possible expressions.

The idea is to strive to *normalize* the expression of love and compassion regardless of the structure or situation. Imagine the power of such a consciousness – a committed group, of any size, functioning at the level of *The Beloved Community* in prayer, meditation, and service with love and compassion. What kind of effect – seen and unseen – might such a force for good have on the spiritual community itself and on the larger community is serves? Going beyond what is visible, we consider the invisible nature of creating an energetic environment of compassion and connection.

"Do all the good you can. By all means you can. In all the ways you can. In all the places you can. At all the times you can. To all the people you can. As long as you ever can."
~ John Wesley

Let us look at activism relating to social justice in this context. I realize that each spiritual community has its own policies and practices regarding all kinds of outreach, and some engage in activism for social justice and some do not. I am using it as an example here of what such activism might look like expressing as *The Beloved Community*.

When individuals or groups engage in activism of any kind, a variety of things about them soon becomes apparent. One is their level(s) on the spiral (see Chapters 4 & 5), another is the degree to which they are embodying love and compassion, another is the quality of their spiritual leadership. How their emotional and spiritual intelligences (EQ & SQ) have been developed is also revealed. And their energy is revealed by the way that they presence themselves in what they do.

When we see groups which are both fundamentalist and extreme on the spectrum of activism, we always see one thing – what they are AGAINST. Indeed, activism is often about protesting something – fighting against something while claiming to be on the side of the Will of God.

Activism within *The Beloved Community* is focused on what you are FOR, such as the capacity to look at injustice and craft a pro-justice message, as an example. While the motivation for activism is usually that something is wrong, the approach of *The Beloved Community* is more about what it would look like when made right. We might ask, "What would it look like if we did not have this problem?"

Another aspect of activism by *The Beloved Community* is that there are clear elements of love and compassion in the message. This does not mean that things are not clearly stated; it does mean that there is a respect for all parties involved. There is no demonization of others, no need to diminish others to make a point or win an argument.

Our nation has seen activism by government and various secular and religious institutions in a variety of guises, but it is almost always against something. We have had wars on poverty, crime, drugs, and so on. None of these "wars" have resulted in "victory." This is not just being kind – although it is always better to be kind – it is the realization of what is effective. Being against something and waging war on it, or on the people involved, is not effective. It is a never-ending process that drains resources and often destroys lives. The way forward is the way of the compassionate heart.

Instead of a war on poverty, we could have had a program for abundance. The name of the program contains what you want, not what you do not want. Psychologically, you are working toward something, not away from it. It seems simple, but it is powerful. Remember, energy follows attention. And energy is directed by *intention*. The intentions of leadership and the community as a whole direct the expression of energy toward a vision – or away from one.

If someone tells me what she is against, I will ask her what she is for. Until she knows that, she is not ready for change. Until she is ready for change, she will not generate change – at least not the change that she desires.

Practicing avoidance, or being motivated by what you do NOT want to happen, is not the way to grow in a positive manner. It does not help anyone find and express their passion in the way that being FOR something does. Being against something does not generate passion; it generates anger. And without passion, there is no energy to carry us and our spiritual communities beyond the inevitable obstacles which arise on any path forward. And it is exhausting to be angry all the time.

"Working hard for something you don't care about is called stress. Working hard for something you care about is called passion."
~ Simon Sinek

Those expressing as *The Beloved Community* speak from what is possible, not from what is unsatisfactory. They speak from the solution, not the problem. They carry a vision forward; they do not spend energy trying to eradicate something negative. They encourage the emergence of our best future, not a retreat to an uneven past. They know that what is emerging will replace what does not work without a fight; it will simply be obvious that it is a better way to be.

This takes spiritual maturity, spiritual poise, and spiritual muscle. The world of outreach often includes those who possess none of these qualities, and as a result, outreach and social activism efforts are often ineffective and can even be destructive. Those doing outreach, especially in areas which are controversial, must be strong enough, have sufficient EQ and SQ, to face the drama and disharmony while remaining centered in spiritual principles – centered in love and compassion. Otherwise, they can do more harm than good.

"Our unwillingness to see our own faults and the projection of them onto others is the source of most quarrels, and the strongest guarantee that injustice, animosity, and persecution will not easily die out."
~ C. G. Jung, Depth Psychology and Self-Knowledge

Only when one has done his spiritual work at a deep level can he be aware of his own projections, and he must work to become relatively free of them. When we unconsciously project our unhealed wounds onto others, we usually make the situation worse. We are easily triggered emotionally and descend into arguments, demonization, and become ineffectual in helping the cause we are trying to support.

The Beloved Community sends spiritual warriors into such situations; people who are strong, clear, and compassionate because of the inner work they have done and the community practices in which they have engaged. These people are ready for outward expression, having waged the battles within themselves to transform from fear to love and compassion.

What does a spiritual warrior do? She looks you in the eye when you are expressing fear and ignorance and tells you that you are better than this – that you ARE love and are capable of being a loving presence, a force for good, and an example to others. She carries an energy of love, peace, and power within her, which she presences wherever she goes. She stands tall in the face of those in fear, and she calls forth her inner reserves of strength, love, and wisdom, bringing them to bear on disharmony and discord. She also uses discernment to pick and choose how and where to use her energies. She does not engage in every battle.

"To be a warrior is not a simple matter of wishing to be one. It is rather an endless struggle that will go on to the very last moment of our lives. Nobody is born a warrior, in exactly the same way that nobody is born an average man. We make ourselves into one or the other."
~ Carlos Castaneda

Spiritual outreach can be many things – feeding the hungry, helping the poor, programs for children to prepare them for educational success, helping the elderly, providing job training, marching for peace or equality, seeking revised zoning laws, working in prisons, and much more. Because of the principles espoused within *The Beloved Community*, a visionary perspective is brought to all outreach efforts — a focus on what is desired, not on what is wrong or absent. This empowering approach becomes an attractor for people who truly want to be involved in making a difference for the better in the world.

These kinds of activities may not be controversial in and of themselves. But social justice issues often are. There are many spiritual communities who refrain from entering the arena of social justice, either because it tends to have political overtones, or because their aim is to be inwardly focused, or because they fear being in controversy.

My question is this — *how many of the great spiritual leaders, whom we revere and sometimes even consider to be divine, have turned away from controversial things?* How many were not engaged in some form of social justice? Can the soul allow us to stay away from serving the world?

"Once the soul awakens, the search begins and you can never go back. From then on, you are inflamed with a special longing that will never again let you linger in the lowlands of complacency and partial fulfillment. The eternal makes you urgent. You are loath to let compromise or the threat of danger hold you back from striving toward the summit of fulfillment."
~ John O'Donohue, Anam Cara

Our world, the human element of it anyway, is crying out in pain for healing. In many ways, we have lost our way on a grand scale. We bicker, fight, cheat, steal, conquer, starve, do great harm to nature and our environment, and often laugh at the results. But our souls call for something different.

Our collective human soul is saying ENOUGH! It is calling forth those who are willing to enter the fray – not to bicker or demonize, but to love, to connect, to enlighten, to heal. Such work takes serious preparation as I have stated again and again in this book. We need *The Beloved Community* to arise over and over again – to bring awakening, healing, and empowerment to more and more people.

> *"Injustice anywhere is a threat to justice everywhere. We are caught in an inescapable network of mutuality, tied in a single garment of destiny. Whatever affects one directly, affects all indirectly."*
> *– April 16, 1963, Martin Luther King, Jr., Letter from a Birmingham Jail*

The concept of *sacred disruption* is an apt one here. The idea of calling upon deep spiritual principles which then are ingrained through spiritual practice can lead to "disruption." The idea is to disrupt the level of thinking and belief that is currently embodied and to create space for a new, higher, more spiritually-attuned level of thinking and belief to emerge.

Once that happens, action can arise from this new level – action that will be from a higher base of spiritual realization than before. This is a key role of a spiritual leader – to facilitate this disruption and the emergence into the new level of love and compassion. Sacred disruption can occur within an individual, a group, a spiritual community, or an entire society.

Whether you call it action for social justice or call it spiritually motivated social activism, it must come from a deep calling that has been seasoned with extensive spiritual practices over time. You might say this desire is to deepen our spiritual realization and then to work toward a vision of creating *a world that works for everyone*. Sacred disruption calls us to move from being children of God to adults of God. We rise and take our place to stand for something we truly believe in and are willing to support, and we bring the best versions of ourselves to it.

Vision without execution is just hallucination."
~ Thomas Edison

"Action without prayer/meditation leads to exhaustion.
Prayer/meditation without actions leads to self-absorption."
~ Jim Rosemergy

As I said in Chapter 1:

The Beloved Community is a collection of individuals who are learning how to love themselves, one another, and the universe. Regardless what name we give this idea, it is the same thing — the creation of the experience of belonging and experiencing the wonders of who we are individually and collectively. It is a place where purpose and passion meet, where we practice being the person we desire to be and support others in that effort. The Beloved Community is a strong attractor to those who seek spiritual realization. It is not a place of struggle but of continual progress toward a vision. That progress may have its ups and downs, but there is a sense of forward motion and of being involved in something vital.

We have reached this final point in the book, which hopefully finds you at a place of greater self-understanding or at least a place where you can accept the need to develop such an understanding. Perhaps you have a better sense of the way forward as a spiritual leader, whatever the form or denomination in which that role exists. To me, the role of spiritual leader in our rapidly evolving culture is to be one who has done extensive personal spiritual practices and is, therefore, capable of being effective in leading others to their own sense of deep spiritual realization. Thus, they may be a force for greater good in this world.

This is a calling of the soul within each of us to be an agent of spiritual healing for humanity even if only for an exceedingly small slice of it.

"Deep calls to deep
in the roar of your waterfalls;
all your waves and breakers
have swept over me."
~ Psalm 42:7

Deep is calling each of us to heed its call – to fulfill our promise and potential as spiritually mature adults. This calling is intended to disrupt old patterns of thought and behavior that do not serve our soul's longing for connection, love, and compassion. And to develop our innate capacities to live as mature adults with a deeper sense of spiritual poise and strength. Ours is a call to awaken our inner genius and to apply it compassionately to the world in which we find ourselves is the clay from which we will build our collective future. Those of us in spiritual community are involved in something vital; it is up to us to ensure that this vitality is not wasted, but is expressed powerfully in our actions. She is ready for change.

"You cannot hope to grow spiritually unless you are prepared to change. Those changes may come in small ways to begin with, but as you move further and further into the new, they will become more drastic and vital. Sometimes it needs a complete upheaval to bring about a new way of life. But it is amazing how soon you can get used to change as long as you have the courage and conviction that the changes which are in place are all for the very best. Let perfection always be your aim. Keep stretching. Keep reaching up to the seemingly impossible. Keep growing in wisdom and understanding and never at any time be content to remain static. There is always something new and wonderful to discover in this life, so expand your consciousness and your imagination to make room for it. Keep open and receptive so you miss nothing."
~ Eileen Caddy

There is no one way to heal the world, no single pathway forward. There are a multitude of good deeds to be done, doors to be opened, old beliefs to challenge, lives to improve. *The Beloved Community* is a name for groups of spiritual warriors who are doing the deep work of spiritual preparation and contributing to the expression of the greater good. They seek to bring the revelation of their souls to bear on the problems of this world — problems that we all share. Simply having the intention to become such an expression is a powerful tool for good.

Everyone in *The Beloved Community* at the local level is doing his or her spiritual work to prepare themselves to make a difference. Collectively, as local communities do their work, they are contributing to an overall effort that we may call The *Universal Beloved Community*. The work of that community is never completed, as spiritual work and service is an ongoing effort as humanity evolves.

Our choices are made within each mind and heart. The calling together of spiritually engaged people into *The Beloved Community* is important work and is essential to the ongoing development of humanity as a species. We are intentionally working toward a better version of ourselves. That better version is within each of us and all of us as pure potential. May we realize it more and more and, together, create something like heaven on earth.

"You cannot swim for new horizons until you have the courage to lose sight of the shore."

~ William Faulkner

BIBLIOGRAPHY & RECOMMENDED READING

I am listing titles and authors here. Everything can be found using search engines in the reading format that you desire.

General Reading for Spiritual Leaders

A Testament of Hope: The Essential Writings and Speeches of Martin Luther King, Jr., by Martin Luther King, Jr. and James M. Washington

Howard Thurman: Essential Writings, by Howard Thurman

The Emerging Church, by Bruce Sanguin

Integral Christianity, by Paul R. Smith

Muslim Clergy in America: Ministry as Profession in the Islamic Community, by John H. Morgan

Sacred Strategies: Transforming Synagogues from Functional to Visionary, by Isa Aron, Steven Cohen, Lawrence Hoffman, and Ari Kelman

Integral Spirituality, by Ken Wilber

The Perennial Philosophy, by Aldous Huxley

Praying Dangerously, by Regina Sara Ryan

Leadership

Presence, by C. Otto Scharmer, Joseph Jaworski, Peter Senge, and Betty Sue Flowers

Theory U (second edition), by C. Otto Scharmer

Reinventing Organizations, by Frederic Laloux

The Resonant Leader, by Anne McKee and Richard Boyatsis

Primal Leadership, by Daniel Goleman and Richard Boyatsis

Igniting Inspiration: A Persuasion Manual for Visionaries, by John Marshall Roberts

Polarity Management, by Barry Johnson

Mistakes Were Made, But Not By Me, by Carol Tavris and Elliott Aronson

Cultural Evolution

Spiral Dynamics, by Don Beck and Christopher Cowan

SQ21: The 21 Skills of Spiritual Intelligence, by Cindy Wigglesworth

Developmental Innovation, Tom Christensen editor

Innovative Development, Tom Christensen editor

A Brief History of Everything, by Ken Wilber

Shadow Work & Psychological Growth

The Dark Side of the Light Chasers, by Debbie Ford

Meeting The Shadow, Connie Zweig & Jerimiah Abrams editors

Spiritual Wholeness for Clergy, by Donald Hands and Wayne Fehr

A Little Book on the Human Shadow, by Robert Bly

Integral Psychology, by Ken Wilber

ABOUT THE AUTHOR

Jim Lockard has been an ordained minister for over 20 years, served on the international board of directors of a spiritual organization and on the boards and advisory councils of several non-profits. Jim received his Doctorate of Religious Science in 2008. He was in pulpit ministry for 20 years in Maryland, Florida, and California.

Jim is the author of *SACRED THINKING: Awakening to Your Inner Power* (2010), and has authored chapters in several spiritual and leadership books.

He is perhaps best known for his blog on spiritual leadership: ***NewThoughtEvolutionary.Wordpress.com***.

Jim retired from pulpit ministry in early 2015 and has been traveling the world with his wife, Dorianne Cotter-Lockard, while speaking and working with spiritual communities along the way. If you would like Jim to work with your leadership and/or membership, just get in touch.
You can reach Jim:
  - ➤ via his author website: JimLockard.Wordpress.com
  - ➤ or at his Facebook Page – Jim Lockard Author
  - ➤ and follow him on Twitter - @JimLockard
  - ➤ Look for and use the hashtag: *#TheBelovedCommunity*

Made in the USA
Middletown, DE
27 May 2017